GOD, HEROES, AND EVERYDAY DRAGONS

FINDING YOUR STORY IN GOD'S STORY

Lifeway Press®
Brentwood, Tennessee

ISBN 978-1-0877-8630-8
Item 005842570
Dewey Decimal Classification Number: 230
Subject Heading: RELIGION / CHRISTIAN MINISTRY / YOUTH

Printed in the United States of America.

Student Ministry Publishing
Lifeway Resources
200 Powell Place, Suite 100
Brentwood, TN 37027

Editorial Team

Ben Trueblood
Director, Student Ministry

Karen Daniel
Editorial Team Leader

Kyle Wiltshire
Content Editor

April-Lyn Caouette
Production Editor

Shiloh Stufflebeam
Graphic Designer

TABLE OF CONTENTS

"We have come from God and inevitably the myths woven by us, though they contain error, will also reflect a splintered fragment of the true light, the eternal truth that is with God."

– J. R. R. Tolkien [1]

ABOUT THE AUTHORS

MIKE BLACKABY

Mike is a pastor and church planter who lives on Vancouver Island in British Columbia, Canada. He holds a PhD in Apologetics and has co-authored several books with his brother Daniel. He loves fantasy novels, playing music, and anything lemon flavored. Mike and his wife, Sarah, have four kids, four chickens, and one dog.

DANIEL BLACKABY

Daniel is a lifelong lover of stories (particularly if dragons are involved) and is the author of multiple books, including several works of imaginative fiction. Driven by a love of movies and stories, he launched The Collision (thecollision.org), a multi-media ministry aimed at helping Christians navigate, engage, and contribute to pop culture. He holds a PhD in Christianity and the Arts from the Southern Baptist Theological Seminary and currently lives near Atlanta, Georgia, with his wife, Sarah, their twin boys, a scruffy dog named Bilbo, and way too many books.

INTRODUCTION

Before You Begin Your Journey

Come with us on a journey. The road we will travel is not just a nature trail. Our adventure is nothing less than the greatest story ever told, and you—yes, you—are a part of it. As with all journeys, you never know what you will encounter along the way. There will be moments of excitement, perseverance, and self-discovery. Some days you might want to quit; other times you won't be able to press on fast enough. That's the nature of journeys; it's what makes completing them so rewarding. Journeys change people. They transform the most unlikely characters into heroes. And this journey has the potential to change you, too. Are you ready?

What Is the "Hero's Journey"?

Years ago, a man named Joseph Campbell developed a famous theory that all stories across all cultures are just reflections (in part or full) of one universal story: the hero's journey. You may not have heard of it, but you've almost certainly encountered it before. Probably many times. The story goes like this: Unlikely characters receive a call to leave their familiar home and enter a strange new world filled with danger and potential reward. Along the way, they meet wise mentors and faithful allies. They overcome obstacles that shape them into the people they need to be to achieve victory for themselves and the world around them. Finally, they return home from the journey, no longer the same people they were when they left. They've become heroes.[2]

Characters such as Frodo Baggins, Mulan, Luke Skywalker, Dorothy (from the *Wizard of Oz*), Iron Man, Harry Potter, Cinderella, Sherlock Holmes, Simba, Moana, and countless others have embarked on different versions of this epic adventure.

The Journey Ahead

Despite what some people believe, the Bible is not just a boring book about things that happened a long time ago or an ancient rulebook we must try to follow. Neither is it a fairytale containing good moral lessons. The reality of the Christian faith is far more thrilling.

The Bible is an exciting, unified story about a real God and real people. It describes where we came from, what went wrong, and how God fixed it. It is an account of how God used a collection of ordinary men and women to start a movement that—despite opposition—spread around the world. It is a narrative of good and evil, companionship, betrayal, violence, romance, and supernatural encounters. It is the greatest story ever told—and you are one of the characters.

An Important Distinction

While you most certainly are on a journey, you are not the hero of your story—that role is reserved for Jesus alone. He is the one who gave His life so we might live. Apart from Him, we can do nothing (see John 15:5). However, in this book we will use the framework of the hero's journey to reveal the path Jesus has you on and how He can continue to shape you as you follow Him.

HOW TO USE THIS BOOK

Over the next fifty-eight days, we want to explore this story with you and help you discover your place in it. Each day is divided into three unique sections:

EXPLORE: How is the hero's journey reflected in the Bible?

DISCOVER: How does this journey reveal your place in that story?

ACT: How can you put these biblical truths into practice?

Journeys are unpredictable. The road will be long and winding. If you fall behind, don't give up. If you miss days, don't grow discouraged— simply pick up where you left off. The primary goal is to finish the journey, no matter what detours you take along the way.

At various stages, you will pause to rest and look back on how far you've come. The end of each section contains a special video message from us that will encourage and help you to complete your own character profile. This activity is also available for download at: lifeway.com/godheroesdragons.

The character profile is designed to provide a summary of your journey. It will allow you to look back on what you have learned so you can continue to move forward to new adventures.

Your life is part of a bigger story. Are you ready to travel together? The road ahead beckons, and your hero's journey awaits . . .

HOW TO WATCH THE VIDEOS

This Bible study has ten free videos that complement the content and launch discussion. You can stream the video teaching sessions any time by going to **lifeway.com/godheroesdragons** or watch them via the Lifeway On Demand app on any Smart TV or mobile device.

Scan the QR codes to download the app!

iOS
Apple App Store

Android
Google Play Store

From the app there are several ways to find our student studies:
- Search directly for the study in the search bar of the app.
- From the Home screen, scroll down. From the carousel for Bible Studies, select View All.
- From the Drop-down menu, select Bible Studies, scroll down to Teen Bible Studies, and View All.

 You can also watch the video teaching sessions by visiting **lifeway.com/godheroesdragons** or scanning the QR code.

QUESTIONS? WE HAVE ANSWERS!
Visit support.lifeway.com, or call our Tech Support team at 866.627.8553.

Day 1

PROLOGUE: YOUR LIFE AS A STORY

I also saw the dead, the great and the small, standing
before the throne, and books were opened. Another book was
opened, which is the book of life, and the dead were judged
according to their works by what was written in the books.
— Revelation 20:12

EXPLORE

W e all love a good story.

Humans have been sharing stories for a long time. Ancient cave paintings depicted feats of bravery and victory. These tales were recited around campfires and passed down through generations. Written language allowed people to tell even more stories and, with the invention of the printing press, to preserve them in books. The oldest known written narrative is called *The Epic of Gilgamesh* (2100–1200 BC), which includes many of the same themes and plot elements found in later stories, such as an account of a "great flood." These days, the most prevalent forms of storytelling are film, television, social media, and video games. Technology has changed, but humans continue to tell stories.

Stories are powerful. People have always used narratives as a way to understand their place in the world. But our fascination with storytelling goes even deeper. Did you know that psychologists have discovered that people view their life largely in terms of an unfolding story? For instance, after a big decision, we say things like, "I'm excited for the next chapter," or "I'm closing the book on that relationship."

> *Life is a journey, and the story of your life will be written according to what you do along the way.*

Here's an exciting reality: Whether you realize it or not, you are in the middle of an amazing story that is playing out all around you. God has been telling this tale since the beginning of time, and it will continue long after the curtain has closed on your own time on earth. Have you ever thought about life like that? We will only discover our true identity and purpose by understanding ourselves in the context of God's incredible story.

At one point in the Bible, Hagar, a runaway slave who suffered unjust treatment, found herself in the middle of a desert, feeling alone and hopeless. While she was there, an angel appeared to her and asked two important questions: "Where have you come from and where are you going?" (Gen. 16:8). Through the angel, Hagar discovered that her life wasn't meaningless. It was a journey, and her story wasn't over yet. God knew her and had a plan for her life.

The same is true for you. Wherever you currently find yourself, you have come from somewhere, and you have a path ahead of you. Life is a journey, and the story of your life will be written according to what you do along the way.

The last book of the Bible includes a fascinating picture. The author of Revelation describes a great vision he received from God. In it, he sees a "book of life" in heaven, as well as other open books. The stories of each person's life are written on the pages of these heavenly books. One day, all of us will give an account to God for the deeds recorded in those books (see Rev. 20:12).

Your life story is unfolding. As Samwise Gamgee asked Frodo in *The Lord of the Rings*, "I wonder what sort of tale we've fallen into?"[3] Great question. Let's embark on this journey and find out together.

DISCOVER

The angel asked Hagar two simple questions: "Where have you come from?" and "Where are you going?" How would you respond if someone asked you those questions?

_____

_____

_____

_____

_____

_____

_____

_____

ACT

As you begin the journey through this book, pray this prayer: _God, thank You for creating me and caring about the direction of my life. Thank You for allowing me to be part of the bigger story that You are telling in the world. Please guide me in this journey. Teach me through the verses I read in the Bible and the ideas I encounter in this book. In all of it, help me come to know You better than I did before. Amen._

 Scan the QR code on the left or visit **lifeway.com/godheroesdragons** to watch the video for the Introduction.

PART 1:

THE
STORYTELLER

Day 2

STORIES NEED STORYTELLERS

And being made perfect, he became the author of
eternal salvation unto all them that obey him.
— Hebrews 5:9 (KJV)

EXPLORE

S tories require a storyteller.

Several years ago, an experiment was conducted with the amusing goal of trying to get monkeys to write Shakespeare. Six Sulawesi crested macaques were put in a room with a typewriter. Things didn't go well. The experiment was canceled after a month with the following results: "The monkeys produced five pages of text, mainly composed of the letter S . . . broke the computer and used the keyboard as a lavatory." [1] It seems Shakespeare's legacy is preserved!

No amount of random banging on a keyboard will ever produce a thrilling novel. Likewise, without an author, life would merely be a chaotic series of isolated events. Only if a masterful storyteller weaves events into a unified tale do they take on meaning. Life is a story, and thankfully, the story has an Author.

God is the divine Storyteller. When God inspired the special revelation of the Bible, He didn't give a detailed instruction manual or Theology 101 textbook. Instead, the Bible took the form of a collection of stories: roughly forty percent of the Bible is written in narrative form. When Jesus came to earth, He further displayed God's storytelling nature by spending much of His short ministry traveling around and telling captivating stories (see Matt. 13:34). More than two thousand years later, those stories (such as His parables of the good Samaritan or the prodigal son) remain some of the most famous tales ever told. One of God's preferred methods of communication is through storytelling.

The purpose of these biblical narratives is to point to God as the Author of an even bigger story, one that began at creation and continues today. If life itself is to be understood as a story, and not just a series of random events, then the Bible is God's declaration that He is the Storyteller: "Then God said, 'Let us make man in our image, according to our likeness' " (Gen. 1:26). God is the Author of life itself. He weaves history together according to His designs.

The Bible also reveals Jesus as "the author of eternal salvation unto all them that obey him" (see Heb. 5:9 KJV). Everything Jesus taught points to the bigger narrative of salvation. He didn't simply tell stories about life; He *is* the Author of eternal life. From the beginning right up to now, God has been unfolding the story of our salvation.

Great storytellers earn our trust. We pre-order new books from our favorite authors because we know they will be good. Acclaimed directors like Christopher Nolan and Jordan Peele often don't reveal any information about a film's plot in the trailers. Audiences flock to the theater on opening night because they trust the storytellers behind the camera. Since your life is an unfolding story, then the most important information for you to know is the Author.

Thankfully, the story of what came before and what continues to unfold all around us is not without purpose. God is the great Storyteller, and you can trust Him to continue to unfold His grand narrative in your life.

> From the beginning right up to now, God has been unfolding the story of our salvation.

DISCOVER

Why do you think God chose to use stories to communicate with us? In what ways do stories teach us truth differently than a more straightforward "instruction manual" would?

Do you trust God as the storyteller of your life? Why or why not?

ACT

Keep this prayer in your mind today: *God, help me see the bigger story that You are telling as it unfolds around me. Please help me to trust You as the Author of my story. Amen.*

Day 3

IN THE BEGINNING . . .

In the beginning God created the heavens and the earth.
— Genesis 1:1

EXPLORE

B eginnings are important. The opening of a story acts as a hook to draw people in. Famous examples include, "Once upon a time," "A long time ago in a galaxy far, far away,"[2] "It was the best of times, it was the worst of times,"[3] and "It was a bright cold day in April, and the clocks were striking thirteen."[4] There are many great examples, but the most captivating opening line ever written belongs to the Bible: "In the beginning God created the heavens and the earth" (Gen. 1:1).

These words set the stage for everything else that would unfold. They establish the theme of God's relationship with His creation. God is eternal, which means He has always existed. So the "beginning" does not refer to God's beginning but to the start of the grand story He is weaving. Genesis 1:2 tells us, "The earth was without form and void, and darkness was over the face of the deep" (ESV). This implies that the universe was a blank page, full of possibilities. Then God spoke, and everything changed (see Gen. 1:3). This is the "once upon a time" moment in which the greatest story ever told was set into motion.

What does this story's introduction tell us about its Author? The first characteristic the Bible reveals about God is that He is a creative being and that His creation is "good" (see Gen. 1:4). He is powerful enough to bring the universe into existence from nothing. He is also intentional. God didn't need to create the universe. He wanted to. His actions were intentional and purposeful.

Understanding your role in the story begins with coming to know your Creator.

Have you ever looked at the breathtaking photos of space captured by the world's most powerful telescopes? The images are filled with bright lights, and each light is actually an entire galaxy that human eyes may never fully see. If you were to take a picture of a section of the night sky the size of a grain of sand and then enlarge it, you would see countless galaxies. It's mind-boggling. What possible meaning could your life have in such a vast expanse?

In the grand scope of the universe, we're very small. Yet the same God who created everything is directing your story. Like a polished diamond ring, small things crafted with precision hold immense value. The universe, and our place in it, wasn't an accident. It came into being because God wanted it to. Understanding your role in the story begins with coming to know your Creator.

The apostle Paul wrote that "[God's] invisible attributes, that is, his eternal power and divine nature, have been clearly seen since the creation of the world, being understood through what he has made" (Rom. 1:20). All of creation points to its Creator—to *your* Creator. Every time you look at the beauty of creation, know that the One who made it all has a purpose for your life. The more you come to know the Author, the better you will understand your place within His unfolding story.

DISCOVER

As humans, we tend to be self-centered. Why is it important to start with God rather than with ourselves to understand our own stories?

Everything that exists was created by God. When you look at creation, what does it tell you about who God is as the Creator?

ACT

As you go throughout your day today, observe the beauty of God's creation around you. Take a few minutes to walk outside and appreciate nature. Keep this prayer in mind: *God, thank You for Your wonderful creation. Help me to learn more of who You are by what You have made. Amen.*

Day 4

AN ACTIVE STORYTELLER

*In the beginning was the Word, and the Word was with God, and
the Word was God. He was with God in the beginning. All things
were created through him, and apart from him not one thing was
created that has been created. . . . The Word became flesh and
dwelt among us. We observed his glory, the glory as the one
and only Son from the Father, full of grace and truth.*
—*John 1:1-3,14*

EXPLORE

The advancement in artificial intelligence (AI) technology has led to some interesting results. One fascinating area of experimentation is storytelling. Computer programmers set the parameters, and then an algorithm spits out a new story. These AI creations have included new books in popular series, such as an eighth Harry Potter novel (outlandishly titled *Harry Potter and the Portrait of What Looked Like a Large Pile of Ash*) and even stories written by authors who've been dead for hundreds of years. While amusing, the content of these computer-generated stories is bizarre and nonsensical, suggesting we don't need to fret about AI taking over the world just yet!

Throughout history, people have often believed God operates like those computer programmers. In this perspective, God (or some other higher power) started the algorithm for creation and then abandoned it to run its course without any further involvement from Him. Have you ever thought of God that way? You may look at the world and conclude that it was created, but the idea that the Creator remains actively involved in its progress seems difficult to fathom.

> God remains active in the world, continuing to direct things toward His desired ends.

The Bible reveals that God is not just a distant computer programmer. He not only created the universe, but also, "in him we live and move and exist" (Acts 17:28 NLT). God started the story "in the beginning" (Gen. 1:1), but He remains actively involved as it unfolds. As Jesus said, "My Father is still working, and I am working also" (John 5:17).

In the opening of the Gospel of John, readers are taken back to the beginning of creation. Christians tend to think Jesus doesn't enter the story until Christmas morning, but John reminds us that Jesus wasn't just present at creation—He was the central figure! "In the beginning was the Word, and the Word was with God, and the Word was God. He was in the beginning with God. All things were made through him, and without him was not anything made that was made" (John 1:1-3).

God is the Creator, but He didn't stop there. He went one step further. The Author of the story stepped into creation in the person of Jesus: "The Word became flesh and dwelt among us" (John 1:14). Not only is God still involved in telling the story He began, but like many famous creators and storytellers—from Alfred Hitchcock to Stan Lee to John Favraeu—He stepped inside the tale and became a character. But unlike these Hollywood directors, God's role in His story is no mere cameo or "Easter egg." It's the pivotal moment of the narrative.

God is not the creator just because of a one-off act at the beginning of time. He remains active in the world, continuing to direct things toward His desired ends. When we call God the Creator, we are not only describing what He did but about who He is. He isn't distant, and He hasn't abandoned His story. He has been actively involved from the beginning, and He remains so to this day.

DISCOVER

Why does it matter that God personally entered the story as opposed to directing it solely from the outside?

_____

_____

_____

_____

_____

_____

How does it change the way you live if you understand that the same God who created the universe is actively at work in your life?

_____

_____

_____

_____

_____

ACT

As you go throughout your day today, keep this prayer in mind: _God, thank You for not abandoning Your creation. Help me to see Your activity all around me. Amen._

Day 5

A CAST OF CHARACTERS

Your eyes saw me when I was formless; all my days were written in your book and planned before a single one of them began.
— *Psalm 139:16*

EXPLORE

Stories often rise or fall depending on the quality of the characters. Great authors create compelling and memorable personalities, and the most ambitious stories often include a large cast. *War and Peace*, the Russian classic by Leo Tolstoy, contains 580 characters.[5] When it comes to book series, the total can be even more overwhelming. The *Harry Potter* series contains more than 700 named characters,[6] the *Song of Ice and Fire* books have more than 2000,[7] and Robert Jordan's fifteen-book fantasy epic, *The Wheel of Time*, boasts a staggering 2,782 named characters.[8] Series with broad casts often include a glossary at the back of the book just to help readers keep track of who is who!

Believe it or not, the story God is telling is even more expansive. It's filled with an almost incomprehensible number of characters. Did you know there are more than eight billion people in the world today? God is telling an expansive story with an unfathomable number of characters—and you are one of them.

As avid readers know, stories with lots of characters can often be frustrating. Sometimes it seems like our favorite minor characters get forgotten or written out of the story. Even the most talented human authors can only balance so many simultaneous storylines and subplots. But God—as an infinite and eternal being—has no such limit. None of the characters in God's story were created on a whim, nor does He lose interest or forget about them. Each one was created for an important role. Before each person entered the tale, his or her story was written down in a heavenly book (see Ps. 139:16).

The author of Psalm 139 was most likely David. The Bible tells us he was a shepherd with seven older brothers (see 1 Sam. 16:10-11). Working alone in a field of sheep, the youngest child of eight, he likely felt insignificant. But before he was even born, God had a story to tell with his life. This overlooked shepherd boy would become a giant-slayer and a king (not to mention a prolific songwriter!). Others may have forgotten David out in that field among the sheep, but God didn't.

> God is telling an expansive story with an unfathomable number of characters—and you are one of them.

The prophet Jeremiah experienced the same assurance from God: "I chose you before I formed you in the womb; I set you apart before you were born. I appointed you a prophet to the nations" (Jer. 1:5). The young prophet had his doubts, but God was confident in the story He would tell through Jeremiah's life (see Jer. 1:6-10).

Your own story may not involve battling giants, ruling a kingdom, or speaking God's words to an entire nation, but the same Storyteller desires to be the Author of your life. He sees you and knows you. You are perfectly cast in the role He has for you.

DISCOVER

Have you ever felt insignificant in a world of more than eight billion people? How do you see yourself differently when you realize God knows you and loves you?

If you believe it's true that God has a plan for your life, how will you approach each day?

ACT

As you go throughout your day today, keep this prayer in mind: *God, thank You for giving me life. Thank You for calling me into the story You want to tell through my life. Help me to understand the role I play in this story and to give it everything I have as I follow Your lead. Amen.*

Day 6

IN CONTROL OF THE STORY

We know that all things work together for the good of those who love God, who are called according to his purpose.
— Romans 8:28

EXPLORE

There is a scene in Steven Spielberg's classic adventure movie *Raiders of the Lost Ark* in which roguish archaeologist adventurer Indiana Jones declares he is going to chase down the army of bad guys and retrieve the stolen artifact. When his dumbfounded friend asks how, Indy mutters, "I don't know. I'm making this up as I go." [9]

Christians sometimes imagine God works that way. We picture Him shrugging and saying, "I'm making this up as I go" as He scrambles in heaven to keep up with the craziness of our world. When we encounter unforeseen trials and difficult circumstances, we may assume God was caught off guard just like we were.

Fortunately, the Bible doesn't describe God that way. He doesn't get writer's block. Even though the journey is filled with unexpected plot twists that can be difficult to make sense of when we're right in the middle of the action, the Author remains fully in control of His story. God is moving "all things" to His desired end, and that end is "good [for] those who love God, who are called according to his purpose" (Rom. 8:28). We may not see where the story is headed, but God does.

Mark 4:35-41 tells the thrilling story of a time when Jesus and His disciples were caught up in a deadly storm while sailing across the Sea of Galilee. The disciples panicked and rushed to wake Jesus, who had been peacefully sleeping through the whole thing! With just a few words, Jesus calmed the storm, leaving the shocked disciples to ask, "Who then is this? Even the wind and the sea obey him!" (Mark 4:41).

The best stories often include moments of despair over seemingly insurmountable obstacles. For the characters within the tale, the end may appear bleak and hopeless. Yet for the author who stands outside the story and knows the ending, these perilous moments are opportunities to develop the characters and set them up for miraculous, future victories.

In the *The Two Towers*, the second novel in the *Lord of the Rings* trilogy, Frodo and Sam try to make sense of the hazardous circumstances around them by remembering the famous heroes in their favorite stories: "We hear about those as just went on—and not all to a good end, mind you; at least not to what folk inside a story and not outside it call a good end . . . And that's the way of a real tale. Take any one that you're fond of. You may know, or guess, what kind of a tale it is . . . but the people in it don't know. And you don't want them to."[10] As we live our lives, we don't always know what will happen around the next corner. Thankfully there is someone who always does.

> When your story takes an unexpected twist, take comfort in knowing that God is not caught by surprise.

When your story takes an unexpected twist, take comfort in knowing that God is not caught by surprise. He knew what was coming and has been preparing you for precisely that moment. The Author of your story knows what you will face tomorrow, which is why He invites you to trust Him today.

DISCOVER

In what ways does experiencing difficult situations in life impact your view of God?

_____

_____

_____

_____

_____

_____

How could Jesus remain so calm in the face of such a terrifying storm? How does this story encourage you to face whatever storms might lay ahead of you?

_____

_____

_____

_____

ACT

Think of someone in your life (such as a friend or family member) who might be going through a difficult "storm" right now. Call, text, or message that person today to offer encouragement, perhaps pointing to Mark 4:35-41 for comfort. Take a minute right now to pray for that person.

Day 7

GOD IS A BETTER STORYTELLER THAN WE ARE

"For my thoughts are not your thoughts, and your ways are not my ways." This is the LORD's declaration.
— Isaiah 55:8

EXPLORE

When we watch movies or read books, we typically associate ourselves with the heroes. The protagonist is meant to be our "window" into the story. Not many viewers think, "Man, I really relate to this Thanos guy" (but if you do find yourself wanting to erase half the universe with some Infinity Stones, please seek immediate help!). It's also a natural human desire to seek the director's spot in our own story. Not only do we want to be the hero; we also want to determine what our story should be. In short, we want to call the shots.

This desire for control is the oldest human problem. Adam and Eve ate the forbidden fruit because they wanted to gain wisdom and "be like God" (see Gen. 3:5-6). God had an amazing purpose for Adam and Eve, but they wanted to direct their own tale. They forgot who was meant to be the director and who was meant to be the cast. A promising story in a beautiful garden paradise quickly became a tragedy filled with shame and suffering. They thought they could

> Every time we try to kick God out of the "director's chair" of our lives, we're settling for something far less than what we could be experiencing.

29

do God's job as well as He could. The next chapters in their story reveal how wrong they were.

God's desire to be the Author of the story isn't because He is controlling or petty. He loves us, and He is a better storyteller than we are. He stands outside the narrative and can see everything that led us to where we are today. He knows everything that awaits us on the path ahead. He knows which road will lead to our most satisfying and impactful life.

Years ago, a series of books called *Choose Your Own Adventure* hit the scene. Every few pages, readers were confronted with a set of choices for what the characters should do next. Depending on what readers chose, they would flip to a certain page, and the story would continue with the consequences of that decision. Choose wisely, and the character would achieve victory. Choose poorly, and the protagonist would be dead after just a few chapters!

You may have heard of these books, but you might have never read one. The genre turned out to be a short-lived fad. Netflix and other streaming platforms have occasionally attempted to revitalize the concept, but it hasn't caught on with audiences. Why? While it sounds exciting to direct the story, making countless "wrong choices" and constantly backtracking quickly becomes exhausting. It doesn't compare to the experience of being immersed in a thrilling story told by a master storyteller. Directors like Ridley Scott, James Cameron, Kathryn Bigelow, or Tim Burton know how to guide a story better than we do. It's better for us to get out of the director's chair and enjoy the ride as they work their cinematic magic.

The prophet Isaiah wrote that God's thoughts and ways are higher than ours (see Isa. 55:8-9). In other words, our best ideas will never compare to God's best. Every time we try to kick God out of the "director's chair" of our lives, we're settling for something far less than what we could be experiencing. Will you live according to your own thoughts and ways, or will you surrender to God's power and wisdom?

DISCOVER

Do you believe God is a better storyteller than you are? Why or why not?

_____

_____

_____

_____

_____

Why are we so tempted to be the gods of our own lives? What is one thing right now that you are struggling to entrust to God?

_____

_____

_____

_____

_____

_____

ACT

Pray the following prayer throughout your day: _God, I want to trust You more. Please help me let go of my desire to be god of my own life. I surrender control to You. Amen._

Day 8

WAY STATION

In most journey stories, the weary travelers require stops
along the road, perhaps at an inn with a warm fire and a
hot meal, or in a peaceful glade, or at a protected castle.
Whatever form these moments take, they enable the heroes
to catch their breath, refresh, and look back on how far
they have traveled.

You have reached the first way station on your journey
through this book. There will be similar stops at the end of
each section. We encourage you not to skip these moments.

WATCH

 Scan the QR code or go to
lifeway.com/godheroesdragons
to watch the video for Part 1:
The Storyteller.

Character Profile

PART 1:
THE STORYTELLER

In the space below, write a short bio to describe how you view God as the Storyteller in your life.

You can also visit lifeway.com/godheroesdragons to download and print the Character Profile in one-page form.

PART 2:

THE
PLOT

Day 9

THE BIGGER STORY

"I have told you these things so that in me you may have peace. You will have suffering in this world. Be courageous! I have conquered the world."
—John 16:33

EXPLORE

Stories require a plot. When you open your favorite streaming platform and select a film, you expect something consequential to take place. In fact, you probably chose the movie because of what you think will happen. If you start a *Fast and the Furious* flick, you anticipate some fancy cars driving fast and furiously. If all that happens is that the main character sits in an armchair with a cup of tea and reads a book, you'll probably turn it off quickly!

In the last section, we explored the reality that God is the greatest Storyteller. The next question is, what kind of story is He telling? One of the most comforting truths you could ever know is that God's story has a plot. It has a clear beginning and is constantly moving toward a decisive conclusion. In between those two points, the story includes all the elements of a good tale—companions, conflicts, romance, plot twists, and thrilling action.

How we interpret our circumstances is called our *worldview*. Some worldviews claim there is no overarching plot to life because there is no divine storyteller; instead, we are left to invent a story that makes sense of our experiences. As we explored earlier, our natural inclination is to make ourselves the final authority for the direction of our story. We must ask ourselves an important question: Do we see an overarching plot all around us because we want to see one, or because there is one that we can see reflected in countless ways?

The first disciples recognized that the miraculous story happening around them was no "cleverly contrived myth" (2 Peter 1:16). Christianity isn't a comforting tale created to give people an artificial sense of purpose. Rather, it's the story to which all other stories point. Author C. S. Lewis came to faith in Jesus when he realized this truth: "Now the story of Christ is simply a true myth: a myth working on us in the same way as the others, but with this tremendous difference that it really happened." [1]

> You have a part to play in God's story, but before we get to your own call to adventure, we must first explore the story that came before us.

Jesus saw the plot. He knew what came before, and He saw what was to come. As He told His followers, "In this world you will have trouble" (John 16:33 NIV). The plot of God's story is no children's nursery rhyme. Like all good narratives, there are plenty of conflicts and trials to overcome. Jesus experienced them, and He knew His followers would too. Thankfully, Jesus also understood the part He played in the story. He decisively faced the sin of the world and came out victorious. He could confidently say, "Take heart! I have overcome the world" (16:13 NIV).

You have a part to play in that story, but before we get to your own call to adventure, we must first explore the story that came before us. Consider this next section the "previously on . . ." recap, like the ones that play before a new episode of your favorite show. Your own story matters, but it must first be understood in relation to the bigger tale God has been unfolding since the beginning of time.

DISCOVER

If there were no God, how would be we able to make sense of the "plot" we see unfolding around us?

_____

_____

_____

_____

_____

In what ways did Jesus "overcome" the world? How does this understanding change the way you see your trouble?

_____

_____

_____

_____

_____

ACT

Today, make a note of at least one "plot point" that helps you recognize the bigger story surrounding your life. Keep this prayer present in your mind throughout the day: _God, when I'm tempted to be overwhelmed by the trouble in my life, help me to remember that Jesus overcame the world and to live in that victory. Amen._

Day 10

"HOW IT STARTED . . ."

So God created man in his own image; he created him in the
image of God; he created them male and female. . . . God saw all
that he had made, and it was very good indeed. Evening
came and then morning: the sixth day.
— Genesis 1:27,31

EXPLORE

Many stories begin with the heroes in a place of comfort until something disrupts their tranquility. In *Avatar*, the Na'vi live in peaceful harmony with their world until an army arrives to harvest their resources.[2] In *Jurassic Park*, humans appear to have everything ready to enjoy their expensive dinosaur zoos until one person makes a bad decision, and suddenly, everyone becomes a tasty snack for a hungry *T. rex*.[3]

It's not surprising that so many stories share a similar premise, since it points to the beginning of our own story as humans. The book of Genesis tells of Adam and Eve living in a beautiful garden paradise. They were God's most important and beloved creations, meant to inhabit the world and enjoy the splendor of what He had made.

The Bible says they were made in the "image of God" (Gen. 1:27), which sets them apart from the rest of creation. They were to act as God's representatives. God is the King of creation, but humans were to have the special responsibility of helping Him rule over it (see Gen. 1:28). In fact, the first specific assignment God gave Adam in the Bible was to name the animals (see Gen. 2:19-20). This job may sound like tedious busywork, but it reflects an amazing truth. For six days of creation, God was the sole creator. But then

God invited Adam to join in the creative process. God is the King, but from the beginning, He demonstrated His desire to have an intimate fellowship with His creations.

Humanity enjoyed a unique relationship with their Creator, and with that privilege came special responsibilities. They were to rule with a love and care that reflected their King. Interestingly, God placed Adam in the garden "to work it and watch over it" (Gen. 2:15). The original Hebrew words used here are later used in the Bible to refer to spiritual service—worshiping and obeying God's commands.[4] This doesn't mean that Adam was supposed to worship creation, but rather it implies that when humans are fulfilling their purpose, it is an act of worship to God.

> Humans have choices, and those choices have consequences.

The garden of Eden set the scene for the story. Everything was established exactly as God intended. What could go wrong? Well, like in so many stories, the perfect paradise wouldn't last forever. God created humans, not robots. Humans have choices, and those choices have consequences. But before we get to the repercussions of Adam and Eve's actions, it's important to consider how it all started. In God's words, everything was "very good" (Gen. 1:31). It's easy to see the world as it is today—broken and full of pain—and forget that it wasn't designed to be this way.

The Author of this grand story is good, and so is His creation. Our hearts long to return to our original intimacy with Him. The plot of this great story is God restoring His beloved creation to its intended design. When you feel tired or discouraged, think of the peaceful, beautiful garden and take heart: the story is leading back to paradise.

DISCOVER

How does the understanding that you carry the "image of God" affect the way you see yourself?

What does God's invitation to join in His work reveal about how He views His creation? In what ways might God desire for you to continue that special task today?

ACT

As you go about your day, let this be a continual prayer that reminds you of the goodness of God's creation: *Lord, thank You for the goodness of Your creation. Help me appreciate its beauty today. Amen.*

Day 11

"... HOW IT'S GOING"

He drove the man out and stationed the cherubim and
the flaming, whirling sword east of the garden of Eden to
guard the way to the tree of life.
— Genesis 3:24

EXPLORE

Choices have consequences. This universal principle is the foundation of countless video games. Based on the decisions a player makes, the NPCs (non-player characters) that populate the world will often treat the player's character differently. In *Animal Crossing*, neighbors grow more friendly or more indifferent depending on how they are treated.[5] In the Legend of Zelda game *Link's Awakening*, if a player tries to walk out of the store with items before paying for them, the game permanently changes the player's name to THIEF, and that's how their character is addressed for the remainder of the game—a continual reminder of a foolish choice![6]

The dramatic tension in God's story is the result of choices and consequences. The serpent in the garden didn't force Adam and Eve to do anything wrong. Instead, he gave them a choice—obey God's rules or seek to become their own gods. They chose poorly, and their rebellion had consequences that we still feel today. The apostle Paul wrote, "Therefore, just as sin entered the world through one man, and death through sin, in this way death spread to all people, because all sinned" (Rom. 5:12). Through Adam and Eve, sin entered the world, and it never left.

Sin is a barrier that separates us from a loving relationship with our Creator. When we sin, we reject God's authority as King over His own creation and attempt to make ourselves the final judges of our own lives. The problem is that we don't make very good gods! In fact, even when humanity created false gods—such as Zeus and his pantheon of fellow deities—they were inevitably selfish, petty, manipulative, and driven by destructive passions. In other words, invented gods reflect their creators' flaws.

> How can God restore what was damaged beyond repair? It would take a miracle. Thankfully, God knows a thing or two about miracles!

The Bible says that "the wages of sin is death" (Rom. 6:23). Death is the unavoidable consequence of sin. God is the source of life, and sin separates us from that source. This death can be literal, but it's often metaphorical: sin kills relationships and destroys families; it demolishes self-worth and steals happiness.

Being a sinner doesn't mean we walk around kicking puppies and robbing banks. Yet, sin is our default. We may use the title "good" for ourselves, but Jesus would answer, "No one is good except God alone" (Luke 18:19). Sin is a disease we cannot escape, and we desperately long for a cure.

Good stories require conflict. The tension in God's story is this: How can sinful people ever return to their intended relationship with a perfect God? It's a seemingly insurmountable problem. Fortunately, while narratives need conflict, the stories we cherish also include resolution. Often the darkest moments lead to the most outstanding victories.

How can God restore what was damaged beyond repair? It would take a miracle. Thankfully, God knows a thing or two about miracles!

DISCOVER

In what ways have you seen sin damage relationships with God, people, and nature?

What are some ways we try to fix our sin issue on our own, apart from God's intervention? How do these efforts fail to fully resolve the problem?

ACT

Considering today's truths, let this prayer be in your heart: *God, please help me understand the seriousness of sin and how I have contributed to the brokenness of the world. Thank You that sin is not the end of the story. Thank You for loving me even when I mess up. Amen.*

Day 12

THE PURSUIT

"The LORD appeared to us in the past, saying: 'I have loved you with an everlasting love; I have drawn you with loving-kindness.'"
—Jeremiah 31:3 (NIV)

EXPLORE

One reason romantic comedies are so popular is that romance and comedy seem to go hand in hand. Love drives people to do crazy things. Love is the force that encourages heroes to persevere or make great sacrifices. Think of your favorite stories. How many of them include characters who give their life so others can achieve victory? How many cherished stories have "love" as the final answer to the problem?

The Bible was written by many authors in a variety of genres. Unlike other books, we typically don't read the Bible from cover to cover. Therefore, we may have trouble recognizing how all the stories fit together into a unified whole. But at its core, the Bible is a true tale of how God loved people so much that He relentlessly pursued us, no matter the cost. Even though humanity has rejected our Creator, He has never rejected us. For thousands of years, God has been at work, drawing sinners and rebels back into a relationship with Him.

Think about the Old Testament stories you know and how they fit into this theme of God's pursuit. When a great flood cleansed a corrupted world, God saved Noah and his family. Years later, God called a man named Abram (later renamed Abraham) to go on a

> God loves us, and He has never given up on us, even when we have given up on ourselves.

journey of faith. Abraham and his wife, Sarah, experienced the miraculous birth of a child whose lineage would grow into an entire nation. Later, when that nation became enslaved in Egypt, God called Moses to rescue them. When those freed people reached an uncrossable sea, God parted the waters. When the people had no food in the desert, God provided nutrients from heaven. Nothing would stop God from bringing His people into the land He had promised to them.

As the nation grew, people continually fell back into their oldest and most destructive habit—worshiping other gods. Each time, God would raise up a king or send a prophet to call them back. One of these prophets, Jeremiah, recounted that 'The Lord appeared to us in the past, saying: 'I have loved you with an everlasting love; I have drawn you with unfailing kindness''' (Jer. 31:3 NIV).

Even in the best times—when God dwelt among His people—the problem of sin remained. God had instituted a system of offering sacrifices, but this law was only a bandage, a temporary solution to a problem that required far more extensive healing. No matter how many sacrifices the people made, they could never overcome the problem of sin. Viewing the Bible through the lens of God's loving pursuit can help us appreciate some of its more difficult books; for instance, the many laws found in Leviticus might lead us to ask, "Who could possibly live this way?" The answer: nobody. Holiness is an impossible pursuit apart from God. If we insist on being the gods of our own lives, we need only to hold ourselves up against God's law to see how far we fall short.

Thankfully, while humanity may look like a lost cause from our perspective, God's love compels Him to pursue a relationship with us. God loves us, and He has never given up on us, even when we have given up on ourselves.

DISCOVER

Once you recognize that God is pursuing a relationship with you, how does your view of God and His character change?

_____

_____

_____

_____

_____

_____

God has loved you even at your most "unlovable." In what ways does this motivate you to treat other people differently?

_____

_____

_____

_____

_____

_____

_____

ACT

Let this prayer be on your heart today: _God, Thank You for loving me and pursuing a relationship with me even though I don't seek You on my own. Please help me love people today in the same way You have loved me. Amen._

Day 13

A PLOT TWIST

*"For God loved the world in this way: He gave his one and only
Son, so that everyone who believes in him will not
perish but have eternal life."*
—John 3:16

EXPLORE

ood stories build tension until the situation appears hopeless. The heroes are outnumbered and surrounded, or the technologically superior alien mothership is charging its planet-destroying cannons, or the home team is losing late in the game and the clock is ticking down to zero. Then, when audiences are on the edge of their seats and all seems lost, a dramatic plot twist occurs that changes everything.

This plot device is sometimes called a *deus ex machina*, a Latin phrase that means, "God from the machine." In the ancient Greek theater, stage machinery would sometimes literally lower a deity character into the story to solve the problems. Today, the term refers to when something unexpected occurs that dramatically alters the events and leads to a surprising victory just when everything appeared hopeless. In other words, the popular concept of the dramatic plot twist is partially based on the idea that at the most desperate point in the story, the characters require a divine intervention.

In fiction, dramatic plot twists are often criticized for being a little too convenient. Such unexpected salvation seems too good to be true. Perhaps this universal plot element continues to pop up because stories reflect reality, and a dramatic plot twist is the climactic event in our own narrative. In God's story, it seemed as though nothing could ever cure people from the stain of evil. Then

Jesus was born—a plot twist in which God entered the story in a way unheard of in any other religion.

> Jesus went from being a baby in a manger, to a Savior killed on a cross, to a resurrected Lord, and finally returned to the Father after commissioning His followers to continue the story.

Like all good plot twists, the Author had foreshadowed what was to come. Still, few people were ready for it. In fact, many people still can't believe it two thousand years later. But the birth of Jesus was the beginning of the ultimate hero's journey: Jesus went from being a baby in a manger, to a Savior killed on a cross, to a resurrected Lord, and finally returned to the Father after commissioning His followers to continue the story.

As sinners, we were helpless to overcome sin on our own, so Jesus—who was sinless—became victorious in our place. The wages of sin are still death, but Jesus died on our behalf. Is it any wonder why the ideas of sacrifice and resurrection play such a prominent part in many of our most beloved stories? We intuitively understand that something (or Someone) must die and be resurrected to bring victory.

After Jesus's victory, there was finally a path for God to restore what sin had broken. God "gave" Jesus as a gift to us on that first Christmas day, and through Him we gain eternal life (see John 3:16). Jesus's death saved us from having to face the consequences of our sin forever, and His resurrection gives us hope that our inevitable physical death will not be the end of our journey.

Our relationship with God, which had been severed through sin, was mended through Jesus. He died the death we deserved so we could live the life God intended. Now that's a good plot twist.

DISCOVER

In what ways did Jesus become the ultimate hero of every
narrative in the Bible?

In what ways is Jesus the hero of your own story?

ACT

Let this prayer be in your heart today: *Thank You, Jesus, for saving me through
Your death and resurrection. Help me to experience eternal life today as You
intended. Amen.*

Day 14

THE STORY CONTINUES

How, then, can they call on him they have not believed in?
And how can they believe without hearing about him? And
how can they hear without a preacher? And how can they
preach unless they are sent? As it is written: How beautiful
are the feet of those who bring good news.
— Romans 10:14-15

EXPLORE

And they lived happily ever after. That famous sentence is the most cliché ending to any narrative, but it's also misunderstood. It doesn't really mean the story is over. After Cinderella marries Prince Charming, their lives presumably continue, but the full story of their relationship would make a painfully long book or film. After all, a movie's runtime can only be so long before we need to rush from the theater to find the nearest bathroom. In fact, even the biblical authors wrote that if all Jesus's deeds were written down, they would fill endless pages (see John 21:25). Most stories we read, watch, or hear are just highlights of a larger tale.

The same is true of the story God is telling. The pivotal, climactic events of history have already occurred. Jesus died and was raised again, victorious over sin. Those were the big, blockbuster moments. Even our modern calendars are divided by these monumental events. But the narrative isn't over. Your own life story is set in the time between Jesus's resurrection and His return.

Jesus's resurrection made a way for people to return to a loving relationship with Him for all eternity, but not everyone is currently experiencing that victory. Sin has been emphatically defeated, but many people continue in their rebellion anyway, not realizing (or not caring) that they

> The gospel is not good news for just the original hearers; it continues to be the greatest story ever told.

have chosen the losing side. Even so, God continues to pursue people, not wanting anyone to perish (see 2 Peter 3:9). We once stood as God's enemies, but we are now called to be His representatives and spread the good news of His victory.

In the book of Acts, we read the exciting account of the Holy Spirit coming to dwell within all believers, empowering the first Christians to spread the story of what they had experienced (see Acts 2). But they weren't preaching a myth. Peter wrote, "We were eyewitnesses of his majesty" (2 Peter 1:16). Another disciple, John, confirmed, saying "What we have seen and heard we also declare to you" (1 John 1:3). They weren't motivated by self-interest either; many of those early disciples were killed for declaring this story as true. They experienced something so real and important that they risked everything to tell others about it.

The apostle Paul knew the importance of sharing the gospel message. He asked, "How, then, can they call on him they have not believed in?" (Rom. 10:14). He devoted his life to telling the story to those who needed to hear it. But the gospel is not good news for just the original hearers; it continues to be the greatest story ever told.

Just as God commissioned the first Christians to proclaim that good news, He calls people today to keep passing it on. In fact, He is calling you. The story God has been telling since the beginning of time is still unfolding. Are you ready to answer the call, join in this amazing story, and follow Jesus on a mission to spread the good news?

DISCOVER

How do you share the story of Jesus with other people? Why is it easy or difficult for you to spread the good news?

_____

_____

_____

_____

_____

_____

ACT

In the space below, summarize the story of Jesus in five sentences or less. Name someone with whom you can share the gospel this week.

_____

_____

_____

_____

_____

_____

_____

_____

_____

_____

Day 15

WAY STATION

PART 2:
THE PLOT

The Bible provides the important backstory to your own hero's journey.
Summarize the highlights of the plot of the Bible below.

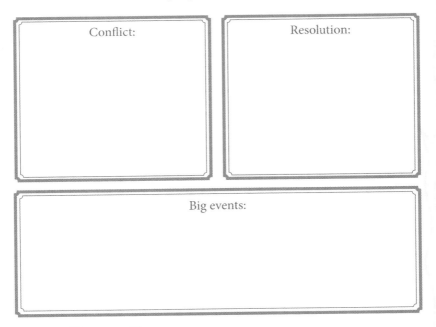

Conflict:

Resolution:

Big events:

Scan the QR code or go to
lifeway.com/godheroesdragons to watch
the video for Part 2: The Plot.

PART 3:
A CALL TO ADVENTURE

Day 16

THE ADVENTURE BEGINS

By faith Abraham, when he was called, obeyed and set out for a
place that he was going to receive as an inheritance. He went
out, even though he did not know where he was going.
— Hebrews 11:8

EXPLORE

In C. S. Lewis's novel *The Voyage of the Dawn Treader*, the Pevensie children and their annoying cousin Eustace discover a painting on the wall that depicts a ship at sea. The image seems to tell a story of adventure and excitement. As they stare at the image, it begins to move and water floods out of it into the room. The children suddenly find themselves pulled inside the world of the painting—the magical land of Narnia.[1] They are outside observers one moment and active participants the next. In the opening sections of our book, we've explored two foundational elements of every story—the storyteller and the plot. Like the Pevensie children, we've been outside observers admiring the painting of a grand adventure. It's time to enter the narrative.

> The path ahead is filled with possibilities, but also the daunting realization that it will require faith and action.

Joseph Campbell wrote, "The hero's journey always begins with a call."[2] This pivotal moment is often referred to as the "call to adventure." It's the event that sweeps the hero up into a bigger world, leaving behind familiarity to embark on a journey. The call comes from a mysterious figure Campbell calls the "Herald" (think Obi-Wan Kenobi, Gandalf, or Glinda the Good Witch) who invites the would-be hero on the adventure. Other times, the call comes not from a person but through an event—called the "inciting incident"— that sets the story into motion (for example, the Reaping for Katniss in *The Hunger Games* or the death of Mufasa for Simba in *The Lion King*). Whatever form the call takes, heroes face a decision: stay where they are or step into the adventure.

The Bible is filled with narratives of characters who answered this call. One of the most famous is the story of Abraham (see Gen. 12). God invited Abraham (still called Abram at the time) to pack his belongings and leave, but God didn't give a ton of details about where the journey would take him (see Heb. 11:8). Calls to adventure are often like that: you don't know what awaits you until you step out onto the path and go.

Abraham would go on to become the father of nations and a foundational figure of the faith. He would experience disappointments and trials but also miracles and victories. He would dine with kings and entertain angels but also wander in the desert. He would see fire rain down from heaven and destroy wicked cities. In perhaps his most terrifying adventure, he would become a first-time father at the ripe old age of 100! His story is one of the most epic journeys in the entire Bible, and people still read about it thousands of years later. His life was many things, but it was certainly never boring! Abraham lived an incredible story, and it all started with answering God's call to go.

Every journey starts with the first step. Something must disrupt your life enough to set you on that road to adventure. Over the next few days, we will explore what happens when God calls you to follow Him on an exciting journey. The path ahead is filled with possibilities, but also the daunting realization that it will require faith and action. God doesn't promise to give us all the details up front. That would make for a dull story! If you never accept the call, then you may never know all that could have been. Are you prepared to respond to the call to adventure? What's your next step?

DISCOVER

What is exciting about a "call to adventure"? What is scary about it? Why might you be tempted to refuse the call?

Think of a time in your life when a "call to adventure" was set into motion. (Did your family move? Did you embrace a new sport? Were you challenged to step out in faith in some way?) How did you respond?

ACT

Let this prayer prepare you for the days ahead: *God, I recognize that You are always calling Your people on new adventures. No matter what fears and obstacles stand in my way, please give me the faith I need to follow You on the road ahead. Amen.*

Day 17

THE WORLD NEEDS HEROES

"Follow me," he told them, "and I will make you fish for people."
Immediately they left their nets and followed him.
— Matthew 4:19-20

EXPLORE

In the second *Lord of the Rings* film, *The Two Towers*, hobbits Merry and Pippen are trying to convince Treebeard (an Ent—a walking, talking, living tree) to join in the fight against the forces of evil. Treebeard and his fellow Ents aren't interested in conflict. They would rather live their comfortable, slow-paced life in the forest. In desperation, Merry exclaims, "But you're part of this world!" [3]

The call to adventure isn't just for the hero's benefit. It's usually extended when a crisis occurs in the outside world that requires attention. Whether it's the classic story of "knight needs to rescue the captured princess," or the Western-movie favorite, "Someone needs to clean up this town from the bandits," the hero's call is an invitation to help others. The hero may benefit along the way, but the adventure will ultimately impact many more people. There is a need, and the hero must step up.

One of the most famous invitations to adventure offered in the Bible was when Jesus approached two brothers named Andrew and Simon (later called Peter) and said, "Follow me . . . and I will make you fish for people" (Matt. 4:19). These men were fishermen by trade; they likely didn't know how to do anything else. Their father was presumably a fisherman, and they probably thought their own children would carry on the family business one day. There's nothing wrong with fishing, but Jesus had far more for them to experience. He wanted them to join a mission that would turn the world upside down.

The fishermen knew how to catch fish, so Jesus used something familiar to help them understand the task ahead. They would "catch" people. Jesus wasn't implying that they should wait outside someone's house with a net, ready to pounce. God was drawing people into His plan of salvation, and He wanted to use Peter and Andrew as part of that mission. The fish they had been catching were temporary; the people they could reach were eternal.

Notice that right before calling the brothers to follow Him, Jesus miraculously gave them the biggest catch of fish they had ever seen (see Luke 5:1-11). Jesus certainly had the power to make them the most successful fishing operation in Galilee. Instead, He invited them to leave everything behind to join God's mission, and they walked away from the familiar to follow Jesus into the unknown. People needed to know Jesus, and Peter and Andrew would be the messengers of that good news. Just as Jesus called them, they would invite others to be disciples of Jesus.

> God placed you on this earth— at this time in history—for a reason.

God may not call you to physically leave everything behind like He did Peter and Andrew. Instead, He might invite you to join His mission right where you are. Rather than leaving your school, job, or sports team, He may invite you to join His mission in a new way among your classmates, co-workers, or teammates.

The world today is in desperate need of heroes. It needs Christians who are willing to step out of their comfort zones and follow Jesus into difficult places. Like Treebeard in Middle Earth, you're part of your world. God placed you on this earth—at this time in history— for a reason. Are you ready to fulfill your purpose? How you answer that question will impact the world around you. God is calling you. How will you respond?

DISCOVER

What are some activities or relationships in your life that are routine for you? How would you feel if God called you to leave these familiar things to embrace something new?

_____

_____

_____

_____

_____

Heroes help meet the needs of others. What potential needs do you see around you? What might keep you from answering the call to meet these needs?

_____

_____

_____

_____

_____

ACT

Think of an area in your life where God might be calling you to step outside your comfort zone. Pray and ask God for the courage to follow Him there. Let this prayer guide you: _God, open my eyes to the needs around me. Give me the strength and courage to follow You outside of my comfort zone. Amen._

Day 18

ORDINARY PEOPLE

For it is God who is working in you both to will and to work
according to his good purpose.
— Philippians 2:13

EXPLORE

One of the most famous scenes in cinematic history is in the first *Star Wars* film, *Episode IV: A New Hope*. After the iconic opening crawl, a small rebel spaceship races across, quickly followed by an immense Imperial star destroyer that fills the screen.[4] The size discrepancy between the ships is almost comical. Without any dialogue, the dramatic tension is clear. The good guys don't stand a chance—or so it seems.

Everybody loves an underdog story. One of the oldest tricks for creating a compelling drama is to stack the odds against the protagonist. A sports drama about a powerhouse team that steamrolls the competition on its way to a national championship would be boring. A romantic comedy about a woman who has it all together and easily catches the guy's eye would make for a short film.

> God is not searching for the most talented people; He's looking for the people who will say yes to His call.

A foundational element of the hero's journey is that the call to adventure is typically a summons for normal people to leave their ordinary world. Joseph Campbell described it as leaving the "world of common day" to enter a "region of supernatural wonder."[5] The beginning of the story usually establishes the hero's ordinary life, which will stand in stark contrast to the world the character will soon enter. Neo will go on to be the savior of the Matrix and Rey will defeat Kylo Ren, but they must begin as an unremarkable software programmer and an orphan on a desert planet.[6] Heroes ultimately accomplish incredible feats, but they rarely start out extraordinary. *The Lego Movie* pokes fun at this idea by making Emmett the most ordinary and predictable person imaginable before becoming "the special."[7] Can you relate?

In the Bible, God demonstrates a preference for underdog stories. When Jesus called His first disciples, He didn't assemble an elite team of warriors or brilliant scholars. He summoned ordinary fishermen. God chose Mary, an unmarried teenager, to be the mother of the Messiah. David, a young shepherd boy, was selected to be the warrior king of a nation. Moses offered a whole list of reasons why he was unqualified for God's mission. He started by saying, "Who am I that I should go to Pharaoh and that I should bring the Israelites out of Egypt?" (Ex. 3:11).

The common thread in these famous Bible stories is not that the heroes were extraordinarily talented or gifted but that they were ordinary people whom God used in extraordinary ways.

Have you ever felt ordinary? Great! You're exactly the type of person God delights in calling. He's not searching for the most talented people; He's looking for the people who will say yes to His call. He is the source of strength, not you: "For it is God who is working in you" (Phil. 2:13). With the power of God at work in your life, you are equipped to take the next step.

When you are tempted to say, "I'm not enough," God says, "My power is perfected in weakness" (2 Cor. 12:9). God loves underdog stories. It is through our weakness that His power is displayed most clearly. Don't worry if you don't feel like hero material yet. How will your underdog story play out? Allow God to lead you out of your "ordinary" world and find out.

DISCOVER

What about you seems too "ordinary" to be special? What excuses come to mind for why you can't do hard things?

Why would God call us to do things that are outside our comfort zones? Why wouldn't He allow us to rely on our gifts and talents?

ACT

Let this prayer be on your mind today: *God, forgive me when I doubt what You can accomplish through an ordinary person. Please help me to see the potential that You see in me. Amen.*

Day 19

CALLED TO FOLLOW

Then he said to them all, "If anyone wants to follow after me,
let him deny himself, take up his cross daily, and follow me. For
whoever wants to save his life will lose it, but whoever
loses his life because of me will save it."
— Luke 9:23-24

EXPLORE

I n the Disney film *Aladdin*, there is a scene in which Aladdin hovers on his magic carpet outside of Jasmine's balcony. He asks her, "You don't want to go for a ride, do you? Get out of the palace? See the world?" Jasmine tentatively responds, "Is it safe?" Aladdin extends his hand and asks, "Do you trust me?"[8] She accepts the offer, and off they go to see a whole new world and sing beautiful harmonies together.

Following someone requires trust. Admittedly, Aladdin isn't the best example, since he's lying to Jasmine about his identity when he extends this invitation! It's important to know who is calling you: God Himself.

Our culture typically honors—even idolizes—leaders. We celebrate people who think outside the box or chart their own paths, sometimes in opposition to everyone around them. The word "follower" is often used as a negative term. The implication is that if you're just following someone, then you are doing something wrong. We like rebels and trendsetters.

Despite its bad rap, learning to follow is an extremely important skill. It can even have life-or-death consequences. In fictional stories, many characters learn this lesson the hard way. Shows such as *Star Trek* depict the disastrous consequences when characters disobey orders. The dramatic tension in many

> Jesus will take you to places you never imagined, show you things you never thought you'd see, and help you experience life in a whole new way.

heist films is often when things go wrong because someone doesn't stick to the plan.

Being a follower isn't a negative thing if your leader is trustworthy. Jesus called His disciples to deny themselves and follow Him because He could lead them down the right path. To "deny" themselves meant surrendering authority over their lives to God. To "take up their cross daily" was a call to commit to Him fully (see Luke: 9:23). In Jesus's day, picking up an actual cross meant there was no turning back on the path towards Roman execution. The disciples had seen hundreds of brutal crosses, so Jesus used this powerful imagery to help them understand the permanence of their decision. What was He preparing them for? To follow Him. The disciples may not have fully understood what the future held, but they knew they could trust the One they followed.

Should you assume God never wants you to be a leader? Of course not. The same disciples who Jesus told to deny themselves and follow Him would eventually become the leaders of a global Christian movement. Yet, in all things, we must surrender to Jesus's leadership. He may appoint us to complete important tasks, but He remains our King.

Aladdin might be a flawed fictional example, but when Jasmine stepped off that balcony and onto the magic carpet, she experienced "a whole new world." What does Jesus have in store for you if you step out and follow Him? Unlike many other leaders, Jesus is completely trustworthy. He will take you to places you never imagined, show you things you never thought you'd see, and help you experience life in a whole new way. Where might He take you? Take His hand and find out.

DISCOVER

Is following easy or difficult for you? Why does our culture struggle to see the value in following?

_____

_____

_____

_____

_____

_____

Have you been hurt or disappointed by leaders in your life? In what ways is Jesus different from those leaders?

_____

_____

_____

_____

_____

ACT

Begin your day by setting aside your normal plans. Instead, ask God to lead you. You can still do the things you have to do (such as school or chores), but instead of being focused on your own schedule, ask God to show you His plans. Then watch to see where He is working all around you.

Day 20

DIFFERENT

"I am not praying that you take them out of the world but that you protect them from the evil one. They are not of the world, just as I am not of the world. Sanctify them by the truth; your word is truth. As you sent me into the world, I also have sent them into the world."
—John 17:15-18

EXPLORE

A recurring motif in superhero stories is the challenge of being a super-powered individual living in an ordinary world. This friction leads to the famous trope of the "alter ego" or secret identity. Superman is the classic example of a character with an alter ego: he combs his hair, puts on glasses, and becomes Clark Kent, a humble—but completely jacked—reporter who clearly never skips "leg day."

The implication of alter egos is that superheroes are different from ordinary people but must try to fit in. They rarely succeed. There is a constant threat of the villains revealing their identities to the world. This duality is what makes the famous ending scene in *Iron Man* genre-breaking, as Tony Stark declares to the world, "I am Iron Man." [9] At that moment, Tony Stark and Iron Man are one. The hero persona is no longer tied to just a suit he wears.

The call to follow Jesus presents a similar challenge. No, you won't need to conceal superhuman strength or X-ray vision from your peers. But as a Christian you are called to be radically different from

> The word "Christian" describes who we are, not just what we do.

the world around you. God also instructed you to be an active presence in the world. In John 17:15-18, Jesus prayed for protection for His followers. He knew the opposition they would face for being different. One of Jesus's disciples, Peter, called Christians "strangers and exiles" in the world (see 1 Peter 2:11). But Jesus wasn't calling them "out of the world" (see John 17:15). The invitation to adventure would lead them *into* the world, but they wouldn't be *like* the world.

It's tempting to approach this calling the same way superheroes do, by dividing ourselves into two distinct personas—our Christian selves and our "regular" selves. We may act one way at church on Sunday but put on our alter egos and try to blend in on Monday. On the other side, we may be guilty of focusing so much on being "different" from the world that we pull out of it entirely. This would be like the Justice League never stepping foot outside the Halls of Justice.

In John 17, Jesus emphasized that He is the example for us to follow. When we read the Gospels (Matthew, Mark, Luke, and John), we see that Jesus wasn't afraid to go where people needed Him. Even though He spent much of his human existence rubbing shoulders with sinners, there was never any question that He was different. Yet He showed genuine love to those whom society deemed unlovable.

The Christian faith isn't something you can put on or take off depending on circumstances, like a superhero costume you wear under your clothes. The word "Christian" describes who we are, not just what we do. If we follow Jesus, then we will be fundamentally different from the world around us.

Will you have the courage to declare, "I am a Christian"?

DISCOVER

In what ways should Christians stand out from the world around us? List one belief, character trait, or action that sets Christians apart from others.

When is it most challenging for you to be different? When is it easiest? Why?

ACT

Let this prayer be on your mind throughout your day: *God, please show me areas in my life where I try to blend into the world instead of representing Jesus. Help me live out my identity as a Christian in a way that is visible to others today. Amen.*

Day 21

FOR SUCH A TIME AS THIS

"If you keep silent at this time, relief and deliverance will come to the Jewish people from another place, but you and your father's family will be destroyed. Who knows, perhaps you have come to your royal position for such a time as this."
— Esther 4:14

EXPLORE

When do we need heroes? We don't require heroes in times of peace and tranquility. No, they usually show up in response to a threat: a dark lord is gathering power, an alien ship appears in the sky, or the zombie apocalypse has begun. Heroes can't exist without a quest or task. If an invading army doesn't march on China, then Mulan never has a chance to save the day. If an evil ring doesn't need to be destroyed, then Frodo lives out his life in the peaceful Shire. If Gotham is filled with law-abiding citizens, then the Bat-Signal never shines in the night sky. A call to adventure is extended when circumstances demand heroism.

Esther is one of the greatest heroes in the Bible. Her journey led her to become queen of Persia. As queen, she could enjoy many luxuries and live in relative peace. Yet, when one of the king's advisors manipulated him into commanding that all Jewish residents be killed, Esther faced a choice: risk angering the king by speaking out on behalf of her people or remain silent. When she faced that difficult decision, her wise friend asked her, "Who knows, perhaps you have come to your royal position for such a time as this" (Esth. 4:14). Esther rose to the occasion, confronted the king, and saved her people.

A hero's journey starts with a decision. The hero learns about a need when the "herald" extends an invitation. The hero must then choose how to respond, and there's often a point when the protagonist resists the call. Understandably so! The hero may experience fear and doubt for numerous reasons. Luke Skywalker initially declines Obi Wan's offer because he believes he is needed more at his uncle's farm. Then the urgency of the situation becomes evident. In Luke's case, the destruction of the farm spurs him to action.[10] In *The Fellowship of the Ring*, Frodo struggles to embrace the call to carry the ring, saying, "I wish it need not have happened in my time." Gandalf replies, "So do I . . . and so do all who live to see such times. But that is not for them to decide. All we have to decide is what to do with the time that is given to us."[11]

> When the world gets dark, God calls Christians to shine a light.

When the world gets dark, God calls Christians to shine a light. Along the way we will face temptations to turn back. We may want to give up. Others might try to lead us on another path. But God calls us to adventure because He knows what is most important. Esther had a choice, but she was also warned, "If you keep silent at this time, relief and deliverance will come to the Jewish people from another place, but you and your father's family will be destroyed" (Esth. 4:14). We must make a choice, and our decision will have consequences.

Will you give in to fear and refuse God's call, or will you step out and go? When you feel tempted to turn back, will you give in or persevere? It's an important decision, because what you choose will affect not only you but many others as well. Trust that God has a plan and purpose for your life. He is calling you "for such a time as this."

DISCOVER

What reasons could you be tempted to refuse God's call? What fears lie at the heart of these temptations?

_____

_____

_____

_____

_____

_____

Can you think of a time when you stepped up and followed God despite your fear? How did the experience make you feel? How did your obedience impact the people around you?

_____

_____

_____

_____

_____

_____

ACT

Pray this prayer throughout your day: _God, I surrender_ (name one of your fears) _to You today. Please help me overcome any obstacle that stands in the way of me saying yes to Your call. Amen._

Day 22

WAY STATION

PART 3:
A CALL TO ADVENTURE

What was your call to adventure? This can be either your the moment you first started following Jesus or the most recent time when you felt God calling you to join Him on mission.

People involved:	Setting (location):

How it happened:	How you felt:

Scan the QR code or go to lifeway.com/ godheroesdragons to watch the video for Part 3: A Call to Adventure.

PART 4:

COMPANIONS & GUIDES

Day 23

COMPANIONS FOR THE JOURNEY

Then the LORD God said, "It is not good for the man to be alone. I will make a helper corresponding to him."
— Genesis 2:18

EXPLORE

Heroes often don't quest alone; their journeys frequently occur within the context of a team or group. Think of the heroes from your favorite stories. What companions did they have? These characters are among the most important in the story and are often fan favorites.

In a hero's journey, there are two types of companions. The first are the guides or mentors. These figures are typically wise or powerful and impart knowledge and hone the skills required for the task ahead. The second group of companions are allies or "side characters." They are usually peers or equals of the hero. They don't possess greater power or ability than the hero, but they typically have skills that the hero lacks.

In most classic stories, the hero has both types of companions. Batman has Alfred (mentor) and Robin (ally). Frodo has Gandalf and Samwise. Lucy Pevensie has Aslan and Mr. Tumnus.

Why do most stories include both important roles? We have an innate need for community. In Genesis, Adam started out alone. Although he was surrounded by animals, they weren't "suitable" for him (see Gen. 2:20 NIV). All throughout the creation account God called what he made "good," but here God recognized that something was "not good."

> Only in community will you achieve what He has called you to do.

Namely, it wasn't good for Adam to be alone (see Gen. 2:18). To fulfill the tasks God set before him, Adam would need help.

God created Eve as a helper and companion. We might think of a helper as an inferior position, akin to a servant or assistant. But the Hebrew word for helper used in Genesis indicates someone with the power, capability, or authority to help, like a powerful ally that arrives to turn the tides of the battle. Often in the Bible, the word is attributed to God.[1] Later, the Holy Spirit would also be called a "Helper" (see John 15:26-27 ESV). In other words, Eve was not merely a lesser side character—she was an equally valuable part of the story God was establishing. Eve and Adam were to be vital allies. Whatever journey God has for you, you're going to need help. Adam and Eve provide a picture of a husband-and-wife relationship, but God may bring many types of allies around you—friends, co-workers, classmates, church members, teammates, and more.

Mary Shelley's *Frankenstein*, widely considered the first science-fiction story ever written, explores the opposite scenario. The monster is alone and deeply longs for companionship, begging his creator, Victor Frankenstein, to create a mate for him. After Dr. Frankenstein refuses, the creature's loneliness drives him to become the murdering monster we know him as today.[2] People were not designed for isolation. From the beginning, God intended for relationships and companions to play an essential role in our journeys.

You have been called to adventure, and you don't travel alone. God has surrounded you with potential guides and companions. Only in community will you achieve what He has called you to do. Over the next few days, we'll look at the people God has placed around you and how they can help you along the path.

DISCOVER

Even the most introverted people long for community. Why are friends and social connections so important to us?

What are some things you're not good at? Can you think of other people in your life who are good at those things? How do their strengths complement your weaknesses? How can your strengths compensate for their weaknesses?

ACT

Today, we invite you to practice this simple action: ask somebody for help. It can be for anything, big or small. Also, pray this prayer throughout the day: *God, please help me use my strengths today to help someone else. Bring someone alongside me who is strong where I am weak. Amen.*

Day 24

A POWERFUL COUNSELOR

"But the Counselor, the Holy Spirit, whom the Father
will send in my name, will teach you all things and
remind you of everything I have told you."
—John 14:26

EXPLORE

D id you know the default position of civilizations throughout history has been religious and spiritual? Over time various populations have drifted into atheism, but every culture has started out with an innate sense that there is a greater power in the universe. Many stories reflect this natural bent toward spirituality. The most obvious examples are the magical elements in fantasy stories or the pantheism in movies like *Avatar* or *Pocahontas*. Also common is a sense of destiny and a belief that things "happen for a reason."

In most stories, the spirituality is ambiguous. Characters may draw power from a spiritual source. It may guide them toward their destiny. But the spirit itself is impersonal. For example, in Star Wars, the wise Jedi Master Yoda said, "For my ally is the Force, and a powerful ally it is." [3] The Force isn't a person. It's just energy. Yoda can't have a relationship with energy.

Some Christians view the Holy Spirit as an ambiguous power we call on in times of need, but Jesus didn't describe Him that way. In the verse above, Jesus used personal, active words. The Spirit is a Counselor who teaches and reminds us.

Countless stories provide examples of mentors passing on wisdom. In the famous dystopian novel *The Giver*, society chooses a young boy named Jonas to be mentored by the Giver. The Giver imparts wisdom to Jonas by transferring countless experiences into his mind (including friendship and love), which their society had lost over time.[4] In *Pinocchio*, the Blue Fairy assigns Jiminy Cricket to be the puppet boy's moral guide and conscience.[5]

But the Holy Spirit is more than our conscience. Jesus promised His disciples, "I will ask the Father, and he will give you another Counselor to be with you forever" (John 14:16). The Spirit would guide them just as Jesus had guided them, and He would be with them "forever." God the Father sent the Holy Spirit to help you on your journey. Jesus promised, "When the Spirit of truth comes, he will guide you into all the truth" (John 16:13). As a person of the Trinity, the Spirit is God with all God's power. When the first disciples received the Holy Spirit, they could do miracles. In fact, Jesus told the disciples that it was better for Him to return to heaven so they could have the Holy Spirit dwell within them (see John 14:17; 16:7).

> The Holy Spirit is working to align you to God's will and to empower you to accomplish every task He has called you to do.

It's important to remember that the Holy Spirit isn't a superpower for us to use however we please. He was sent in the name of Jesus. He isn't interested in helping us pursue selfish goals. The Holy Spirit is working to align you to God's will and to empower you to accomplish every task He has called you to do. In other words, if you aren't willing to follow and obey Jesus, don't expect to experience the Holy Spirit's power in your life.

If you are seeking to follow Jesus, then take heart in knowing that the full power of God dwells within you and will guide you each step of the way.

DISCOVER

Why do we need mentors and guides?

_____

_____

_____

_____

_____

_____

_____

Jesus called the Holy Spirit the "Spirit of truth" (see John 14:17; 16:13). In what areas of your life are you struggling to know the truth? How can you bring them before the Holy Spirit in prayer?

_____

_____

_____

_____

_____

_____

ACT

Jesus said the Holy Spirit would "convict the world about sin . . . because they do not believe in me" (John 16:8-9). Think of someone in your life who doesn't believe in Jesus. Pray for that person to be convicted by the Holy Spirit and turn to Jesus as Savior and Lord.

Day 25

A RELIABLE MAP

For the word of God is living and effective and sharper than any double-edged sword, penetrating as far as the separation of soul and spirit, joints and marrow. It is able to judge the thoughts and intentions of the heart.
— Hebrews 4:12

EXPLORE

A classic element in many quest stories is that the hero receives a map or navigational object. In *Treasure Island*, Jim Hawkins receives a treasure map to Captain Flint's buried treasure.[6] Video games often include interactive maps with markers and highlighted paths to help players cross the expansive worlds. God has also given you a physical, tangible object to direct your path: the Bible.

The Bible is the most influential book in human history. It holds the Guinness World Record as the best-selling book of all time.[7] But although the Bible is a fascinating book, it's much more than just literature. It is a map for Christians. Like Jack Sparrow's "broken" compass in *Pirates of the Caribbean*, the Bible points us to what our heart most desires: God Himself. Like Sparrow's compass, which doesn't point toward magnetic north, the Bible may appear strange or foolish to those unfamiliar with its true value. Yet it is the most reliable navigational tool you have for your journey. Within its pages you can come to know your Creator.

Perhaps you've heard the Bible described as an instruction manual. While its pages do contain helpful guidelines and important commands, it is more than a rulebook. Unlike Jim Hawkins' map, Scripture isn't a lifeless document; in Hebrews 4:12 it is described as "living" (no, not in the same way as some of

Harry Potter's textbooks). Scripture is a channel through which God speaks to us (which is why it is often called "God's Word"). As you read Scripture, the Holy Spirit will help you understand and apply the timeless truths to your own life.

> The Bible is the most reliable navigational tool you have for your journey. Within its pages you can come to know your Creator.

If we have the Holy Spirit, then why do we need the Bible? The prophet Jeremiah once explained, "The heart is more deceitful than anything else, and incurable—who can understand it?" (Jer. 17:9). As sinful people, we are easily deceived. Sometimes what we attribute to the Holy Spirit is really our own selfish desires. Our emotions are powerful, and in the heat of the moment they can distract us from what the Holy Spirit is saying. God inspired the collection of sixty-six books that make up our Bibles today to reveal who He is and how He operates. Scripture "is able to judge the thoughts and intentions of the heart" (Heb. 4:12). When you feel your heart leading you, check it against the truth of Scripture. The Holy Spirit will guide you to the words of Jesus (see John 14:26).

You are not journeying along a single, clearly marked path. Countless trails veer off in many directions, and other travelers will call for your attention. Without guidance, you will quickly find yourself lost in the woods, far removed from where God called you to go. Thankfully, "all Scripture is God-breathed and is useful for teaching, rebuking, correcting and training in righteousness, so that the servant of God may be thoroughly equipped for every good work." (2 Tim. 3:16-17 NIV). A map is only helpful if you use it. Immerse yourself in Scripture and allow God to equip you for the journey ahead.

DISCOVER

What have you read in the Bible that confused you?

What have you read in the Bible that encouraged you?

ACT

Have you ever used the index or concordance feature at the back of your Bible? It can lead you to verses relating to specific topics. Pick one topic you're interested in learning about, and locate that term in the index or concordance at the back of your Bible or search "What does the Bible say about [*your topic*]?" using the internet. Spend some time looking into what the Bible says about your topic. What did you learn? What new questions do you have?

Day 26

BREAKING THE FOURTH WALL

"Call to me and I will answer you and tell you great and incomprehensible things you do not know."
—Jeremiah 33:3

EXPLORE

Imagine you've gone to a theater to see *Hamilton*, *Wicked*, or some other Broadway play. You sit in your seat and look out at the stage. The set design has three walls: one at the back, and one on each side. Obviously, the characters don't act as though they are living in a three-walled house with a live audience watching their every move. The last wall—the fourth wall—is invisible, an imaginary barrier separating the audience from the actors. You can see through it, but the actors on stage behave as if they can't.

Now imagine one of those characters suddenly turns in your direction and speaks to you. That would be an example of the storytelling technique called "breaking the fourth wall." Other examples include times when comic book characters—such as Deadpool and She-Hulk—interact directly with the reader. Even the honey-loving bear Winnie the Pooh occasionally talks to the narrator of his story. In whatever form it takes, breaking the fourth wall involves someone within a story communicating with someone outside the story.

What comes to mind when you think of prayer? Perhaps it's just a few words said before a meal ("God, please bless this greasy fried chicken and salty French fries to the nourishment of my body . . ."). We pray, but perhaps we don't always appreciate how incredible prayer is. In a sense, when we pray, we're breaking the fourth wall. As we live out our life stories, we can communicate directly with the Storyteller. When we pray, we transcend our current circumstances and talk with Someone who knows every detail of the story from beginning to end.

In Jeremiah 33:3, we're invited to initiate the conversation by calling out to God. We're typically pretty good at that part. Now, look at what follows: "I will answer you and tell you great and incomprehensible things you do not know" (Jer. 33:3). Prayer is an opportunity for us to talk to God. Even more importantly, it's a time when God speaks to us. We're not always good at that part. We tend to think of prayer more as "talking" than "listening." While God is pleased when we come to Him with our worries and questions, He already knows all things—and many things we don't. If someone should do most of the talking, it should be God!

> When we pray, we transcend our current circumstances and talk with Someone who knows every detail of the story from beginning to end.

Sometimes frustrated Christians express that they never seem to hear God speak or answer their prayers. Perhaps one explanation is that whenever they spend time with God in prayer, they do all the talking. Prayer involves listening and being on the lookout for how God may be answering those prayers. Prayer is indispensable on our faith journey.

The writer of Hebrews reminds us that Jesus is our "great high priest" (Heb. 4:14). In other words, we don't need another human to be a messenger between us and God; we can speak directly to Him. "Therefore, let us approach the throne of grace with boldness, so that we may receive mercy and find grace to help us in time of need" (Heb. 4:16). In our time of need, it's not enough to rely on what we already know. We need God's grace to tell us "great and incomprehensible things" we don't know. As you travel along your journey, don't hesitate to break the fourth wall often, since you have the amazing opportunity to relate to the Storyteller Himself.

DISCOVER

What are some questions you are facing in your life right now? What are some of the biggest distractions that might prevent you from taking time to be still and listen to God in prayer?

Can you recall a time when you experienced God's clear answer to your prayer? How does remembering that experience give you confidence and peace during times when you are still waiting for His answer?

ACT

Pray and ask God to speak to you. Then take the next two minutes to be still before God and listen. Don't worry if you don't get any lightning bolts through the ceiling of your bedroom! Being still and listening takes practice. These two minutes are just a starting place. Continue this practice each day this week and see what happens.

Day 27

FRIENDS & ALLIES

Iron sharpens iron, and one person sharpens another.
— Proverbs 27:17

EXPLORE

O ne of the most crowd-pleasing moments in recent movie history is the climax of *Avengers: Endgame*. Captain America finds himself standing alone and beaten, confronted by the overpowering army of Thanos. All seems hopeless—until portals start opening all around him, and out marches an army of heroes. His friends and allies have come, and he no longer stands alone. The scene is iconic not just due to the expensive spectacle but because of the meaning. A decade's worth of movies established these characters and developed their relationships. Now, with the fate of the world hanging in the balance, the culmination of those relationships is summed up in two words: *Avengers assemble!*[8]

> It's not about having the most friends but about having the right ones.

Friends and allies are some of the most important characters in your story. The Bible says, "Iron sharpens iron, and one person sharpens another" (Prov. 27:17). No warrior wants to be in the heat of battle with a dull weapon. The biblical imagery is that of a sword being scraped against iron repeatedly, sharpening the edge of the blade so it is ready to perform the task for which it was designed.

Jesus set the example. He surrounded Himself with twelve men as His innermost circle of friends, as well as several close female followers (see Luke 8:1-3). Jesus's relationship with His disciples went beyond that of a teacher to students. Jesus spent many meals with His disciples, and they shared most of their daily activities. In the monumental moments of Jesus's life, such as in the garden of Gethsemane before His betrayal and crucifixion, Jesus often surrounded Himself with His three closest disciples: Peter, James, and John (see Matt. 26:37). Jesus told His disciples, "I do not call you servants anymore, because a servant doesn't know what his master is doing. I have called you friends, because I have made known to you everything I have heard from my Father" (John 15:15).

Your friends influence you in ways you may not even realize. They can have a greater impact on you than just about anyone else in your life. Friends matter, so choose them wisely. It's not about having the most friends but about having the right ones. Will they be there to help you along the path of discipleship? As the book of Ecclesiastes warns, we "pity the one who falls without another to lift him up" (Eccl. 4:10).

Will your friends sharpen you and help you follow Jesus? Do they speak the hard truth when they see you wandering from the right path? In the big moments, are they quick to assemble and fight by your side?

Keep in mind that your friends need sharpening as well. They will play an important role in your journey, but you also play a crucial part in theirs. In a healthy friendship, both participants are enriched and strengthened by the bond. If your friends aren't able to help you on your journey, God may lead you to find new allies. He may also challenge you to set an example of faithful companionship (see Heb. 10:24).

Without quality friends, you are a dull blade and likely unsuited for the mission God has for you. Surround yourself with faithful companions. Good friends and allies will shape you into the hero God wants you to be.

DISCOVER

Who are your three best friends? Do they share your Christian faith? In what ways do they help you follow Jesus?

Think of a time you faced a difficult situation. Did your friends support you during that challenging season? Can you think of a time when you did the same for them?

ACT

Take a few minutes to send an encouraging text to the friends you listed above, or speak to them in person. Think of a way to encourage them in their faith. Perhaps share some Bible verses with them. You may even choose to send them the verse at the beginning of this devotion. Thank them for "sharpening" your life. Pray that they would continue to be sharpened into the people God desires for them to be.

Day 28

AN IMPORTANT FELLOWSHIP

*And let us consider one another in order to provoke love
and good works, not neglecting to gather together, as some
are in the habit of doing, but encouraging each other, and
all the more as you see the day approaching.*
— *Hebrews 10:24-25*

EXPLORE

"We either live together, or we die alone."[9] The television show *Lost* is one of the most popular and influential series ever made. Although the plot became increasingly complex over time—including elements such as mysterious smoke monsters, random polar bears, time travel, and more— the general premise was simple: a plane crashes on an unknown island, and the survivors need to work together to survive. What made the show so compelling for six seasons was the diverse cast of characters and their fascinating relationship dynamics.

There is tremendous value in surrounding yourself with people who are different from you. Friends are important, but our best friends are typically peers who have similar interests. The church is different. Hopefully church members are friends, but the New Testament speaks of the church as a family (for examples, see 2 Cor. 6:18; 1 Tim. 5:1; Matt. 12:50; Eph. 2:19). Unlike friends, we generally don't choose our family. Typically, we're either born or adopted into it. As a "born again" believer, you are grafted into the family of God, which is the church.

Because of its diverse makeup, the church doesn't always get along perfectly. We may disagree or even hurt one another. Yet, despite these differences, we are united through Jesus and our shared mission to spread the gospel.

In recent years, society has lost much of its reverence for the church. Whereas the importance of attending church was once widely acknowledged, now many people—including Christians—question its value, instead embracing a "just me and Jesus" mindset. Part of this negative stigma stems from various abuses and scandals. Another reason people view church as unimportant is because we've lost sight of what the church truly is. Christians shouldn't attend worship services out of "rule-following" duty but because the church makes up our spiritual family.

> We don't just go to church; we are the church.

We don't just go to church; we are the church. Our Sunday worship experience is important, but it's kind of like "family dinner." Families benefit greatly from having dinner together at the end of the day, but their bond isn't solely built on that. There are many other ways a healthy family strengthens their relationships and accomplishes their goals. The same is true of the church. We should develop the habit of worshiping together on Sunday, but we should also find other ways to "stir up one another to love and good works . . . encouraging one another" (Heb. 10:24-25 ESV).

No family is perfect. Siblings bicker, and parents may lose their patience with each other, sometimes to the point of divorce. Because a family contains diverse members, all with different and sometimes competing needs, there is potential for hurt feelings and disappointment. Yet, at the end of the day, family is worth fighting for.

Don't journey alone. Find your fellowship.

DISCOVER

What do you think of the church? Are you part of a local church family? If not, why not?

_____

_____

_____

_____

_____

How might your faith grow as a result of being part of a church family?

_____

_____

_____

_____

_____

ACT

Attend a worship service this week and look for someone to encourage while you're there. Perhaps sit in a different part of the sanctuary than usual and get to know the people in that section, or look for an elderly adult sitting alone and ask if you can sit with her or him. Afterward, be sure to say "thank you" to leaders such as your pastor or youth pastor. It will mean a lot to them. Ask how you can get more involved with your church family.

Day 29

WAY STATION

PART 4:
COMPANIONS & GUIDES

Who is your Fellowship? Think of the people in your life who are currently walking alongside you in your hero's journey.

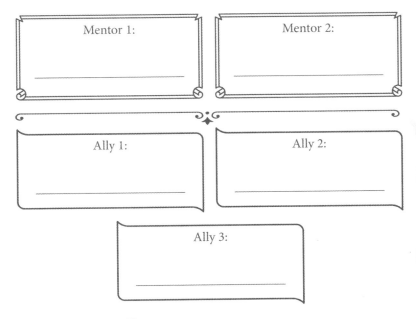

Mentor 1:

_____

Mentor 2:

_____

Ally 1:

_____

Ally 2:

_____

Ally 3:

_____

Scan the QR code or go to lifeway.com/godheroesdragons to watch the video for Part 4: Companions & Guides.

PART 5:

CHARACTER
ARC

Day 30

YOU WON'T BE THE SAME

*We all, with unveiled faces, are looking as in
a mirror at the glory of the Lord and are being
transformed into the same image from glory to
glory; this is from the Lord who is the Spirit.*
— 2 Corinthians 3:18

EXPLORE

"Can you promise I will come back?" — Bilbo Baggins
"No, but if you do, you will not be the same." — Gandalf [1]

Journeys change people. The character who sets out at the beginning is never the same as the one who returns at the end. The idea of growth is a crucial aspect of not just the hero's journey but all storytelling. If the hero remains unchanged, we criticize the story for lacking "character development."

Growth plays an important role in video games too. In many games, players earn "experience points" (XP) for performing tasks, which can usually be spent to level up the character or gain new skills and abilities. Every gamer has experienced the satisfaction of returning to earlier parts of the game and easily defeating enemies that once seemed invincible. Why are these moments so gratifying? Perhaps because the reality of transformation is an important part of God's design for creation.

> We are all heading toward a destination, but most of life happens along the way.

We often compare ourselves to Christians who are further along in the journey, and when we do, we can become discouraged or impatient. We want to be mighty heroes, but we're still clumsy and incapable. Unfortunately, there is no shortcut to character growth. It's through the journey that God molds us into the people He wishes for us to be. There is a saying in Brandon Sanderson's popular *Stormlight Archive* novels: "Journey before destination."[2] We are all heading toward a destination, but most of life happens along the way.

Faith grows through action. When the Israelites fled captivity from Egypt, they ended up at the shores of the Red Sea. With the Egyptian army behind them, all seemed hopeless. Yet, when they obeyed God's command to "go forward" (Ex. 14:15 ESV), they witnessed a miracle as God parted the sea. After arriving on the other side, the Bible recounts that "when Israel saw the great power that the LORD used against the Egyptians, the people feared the LORD and believed in him and in his servant Moses" (Ex. 14:31). God didn't grow their faith while they stood on the shore. It was walking through the sea and arriving safely on the other side that strengthened their faith.

God will shape your faith as you follow Him. The path ahead may seem daunting, but God reveals His power through difficult experiences. If you desire a greater faith, God may put a "Red Sea" in front of you. If you have the courage to walk through it, you will find that your faith has grown by the time you reach the other side.

Sanctification is the term theologians use to describe the process of growing your faith and character over time. Make no mistake: this journey will change you. God is at work in your life, and the result will be incredible. Paul said we are being transformed into the "same image" of Jesus (see 2 Cor. 3:18). As you travel this hero's journey of faith, you'll find yourself being shaped by the Holy Spirit to reflect Jesus more accurately in your character and actions.

DISCOVER

What is the difference between reading or hearing about something and experiencing it for yourself?

What are the most significant experiences you have had with God? How did those encounters change you?

ACT

Think of the person you were last year. In what ways are you the same, and in what areas have you changed? Now look to the future. In which areas do you hope God will grow you? Thank God for all He has done: *God, thank You for helping me grow so I am not the same person I once was. Help me to be patient and willing as You continue to shape me to look more and more like Jesus. Amen.*

Day 31

UNFINISHED MASTERPIECES

For we are his workmanship, created in Christ Jesus for good
works, which God prepared ahead of time for us to do.
— *Ephesians 2:10*

EXPLORE

W hat makes something a masterpiece? Have you ever wondered why some creations are almost universally praised as timeless, while others come and go without making even a ripple? According to some estimates, around four million new books are published each year,[3] yet many of us probably studied the same handful of books in school. There are more than one hundred million songs on Spotify,[4] yet if we attend a sporting event and the home team is losing late in the game, we know we're about to hear "Don't Stop Believing" by Journey blaring through the speakers.

All masterpieces share a common feature: they are excellently constructed by a master craftsman. You may think *Moby Dick* is boring, but a creation's value is not determined by its popularity. Mass-market romance novels are popular, but that doesn't make them masterpieces. *Moby Dick* is recognized as a masterpiece because of the skill of its author, Herman Melville, and the story's timelessness. The same is true of you.

God is the Great Artist. His creation, and the story it tells, has value because of who made it. The word "masterpiece" in Ephesians 2:10 (NLT) is sometimes translated as "handiwork," meaning the skilled work of God's hands. In fact, the original Greek word is *poiema*, which is related to the English word "poem." [5,6]

You are one of God's masterpieces, and He created you for a purpose. As you follow Him on your journey, He will shape you into who He desires you to be. The apostle Paul wrote, "I am sure of this, that he who started a good work in you will carry it on to completion until the day of Christ Jesus" (Phil. 1:6).

Though you are a masterpiece, you are also unfinished. God is continuing to mold and shape you. The Bible puts it this way: "For by one offering he has perfected forever those who are sanctified" (Heb. 10:14). If you are a Christian, God has forgiven you because of Jesus's death and resurrection. But He is still in the process of making your life reflect that freedom.

We see this concept reflected in many stories in which seemingly unqualified characters are chosen for a heroic task. These heroes aren't yet who they will one day become, but they are deemed worthy of the task ahead. Consider the famous tale of King Arthur and the sword in the stone. He is worthy enough to pull the sword from the stone, but it will take years before he becomes the legendary king of Camelot.

> Though you are a masterpiece, you are also unfinished. God is continuing to mold and shape you.

We get the same picture from Scripture. Your life is so valuable that God sent His own Son to die for your sins. The transformation that occurs on your journey is not what makes you worthy of God's love. He already loves you. Rather, He wants to make you more like Jesus *because* He loves you (see 2 Cor. 3:18; Rom. 8:29). A master Craftsman created you; the greatest Storyteller is directing your life. You are an unfinished masterpiece who is both valuable and a work in progress. Allow God to continue His great work in you, and He will shape you into the masterpiece He knows you are.

DISCOVER

What are some things you dislike about yourself? How do these perceived flaws make you feel about yourself?

How does the Bible say God feels about you? How does the truth that you are already a masterpiece and a work in progress comfort you?

ACT

Let this prayer be on your mind and heart today: *God, thank You for bringing me into existence as something of great value. Help me to see myself the way You see me and continue to make me more like Jesus. Amen.*

Day 32

A HERO'S IDENTITY

There is no Jew or Greek, slave or free, male and female; since
you are all one in Christ Jesus. And if you belong to Christ, then
you are Abraham's seed, heirs according to the promise.
— Galatians 3:28-29

EXPLORE

All heroes experience a sense of "self-discovery" on their journey. Buzz Lightyear learns the hard lesson that he isn't a real space ranger; he's just a toy.[7] The four Pevensie siblings must reconcile their identity as the prophesied kings and queens of Narnia with the reality that they're just kids from a different world.[8] Peter Parker is told, "If you're nothing without the suit, then you shouldn't have it,"[9] and he is forced to discover his identity as a hero beyond his Spider-Man persona.

The faith journey involves a similar process of discovery. Adventures push us out of our comfort zones and make us ask hard questions, such as, "Who am I really?" We discover our strengths—and our weaknesses. Our choices shape us. Many classic villains adopt their evil identity in response to difficult life events. As we walk by faith into unknown places, we ultimately face the possibility of finding ourselves or losing ourselves completely.

Today's culture is obsessed with the idea of identity. Arguably the most esteemed virtue today is to be "true to yourself." Of course, we must first know

> Only when our identities are rooted in the unchanging person and work of Jesus do we see ourselves for who we really are.

who we are. Understanding our identity is important, but it can become a selfish pursuit that puts the focus on ourselves rather than on others.

Is it bad to want to understand ourselves? Certainly not! One outcome of any hero's journey is that the hero returns with a clearer self-image. But where we find our identity matters. In a world full of labels (some we've put on ourselves, others have been assigned to us), the Bible offers a radical new understanding of identity. In Galatians 3:28-29, the apostle Paul addressed three attributes that often form the basis of someone's identity: race, social status, and gender. He doesn't deny that these categories exist, but he also emphasized that our true identity is found in something deeper.

Paul wrote, "For as many of you as were baptized into Christ have put on Christ" (Gal. 3:26 ESV). Christ becomes the "label" wrapped around every other identifier we may have adopted. One of the marks of Christian maturity is that we understand ourselves in relation to Christ. Beneath that label, we may possess traits that would otherwise divide us, but putting on Christ unites us as family. Our relationship to Jesus is what matters most, and everything else makes sense in relation to it.

You, like every hero, will see yourself in a new light by the end of the journey. God made you unique. Embrace and celebrate the distinctive aspects of yourself and the people around you. Becoming a Christian doesn't mean we all must look, sound, or think the same. Life would be boring if we did. In John's vision of heaven, he saw, "a vast multitude from every nation, tribe, people, and language, which no one could number, standing before the throne" (Rev. 7:9). Our differences make us unique, but they don't draw us into a relationship with God; only Christ can do that. In the context of eternity, our relationship with Jesus is what matters most.

Only when our identities are rooted in the unchanging person and work of Jesus do we see ourselves for who we really are. We also see other people differently. We look past all the surface labels and see a person for whom Jesus died on the cross.

DISCOVER

Where have you found your identity? Why do the labels you use matter to you? What is the danger of putting too much of your identity in these things?

How does your relationship with Jesus change the way you understand yourself? How does Jesus change the way you see other people?

ACT

Let this prayer be in your heart and mind as you go about your day: *Lord, thank You that my identity is so much more than I often make it. Help me to see myself the way You see me and to view others in light of Your love for them. Amen.*

Day 33

WHAT DEFINES A HERO

"By this everyone will know that you are
my disciples, if you love one another."
—John 13:35

EXPLORE

What defines a hero? Strength, bravery, or a special ability? Many of the fictional heroes we admire possess some sort of superpower (Wonder Woman, the X-Men, Paul Atreides) or an extra dose of human gifts, like intelligence or bravery (Iron Man, Princess Leia, Sherlock Holmes). These skills are obviously helpful in defeating the bad guys, but are they what make these characters heroes? No. In many stories, the heroes' abilities are somehow stripped away (think Superman and kryptonite), leaving them to prove who they are without extra powers.

As the *Harry Potter* books and *Star Wars* films have explored, simply having abilities doesn't make someone heroic. Special powers can be used for evil as well as good. Perhaps the one thing that unites all heroes is their willingness to make sacrifices. We acknowledge selflessness in real-world heroes when we honor service members, police officers, firefighters, or healthcare workers. To become a true hero, a person must sacrifice on behalf of others.

The hero's journey is not a selfish pursuit, even if it begins as a character's longing for adventure. Eventually, even these heroes learn that it is only through sacrifice that they can fulfill their greater purposes. At its heart, the gospel story—the ultimate hero's journey—is the same. The cross is a reminder of how much God was willing to give to save us.

> A good indication that a character is becoming a "hero" is when she or he sets aside personal desires for someone else's good.

Love is most powerfully displayed through sacrifice. Every story that showcases sacrificial love echoes the words of Jesus: "No one has greater love than this: to lay down his life for his friends" (John 15:13). Jesus took things even further: "God proves his own love for us in that while we were still sinners, Christ died for us" (Rom. 5:8).

Of course, demonstrating sacrificial love doesn't always mean literally dying for someone else. It can take many forms. A clear example is when Jesus did the socially unthinkable and washed His disciples' feet (see John 13:1-20). Feet were considered both religiously unclean and just plain gross (walk around on hot dusty roads wearing sandals and you'll see why!). For a respected teacher to stoop down to wash His students' feet was shocking. And that was the point. Jesus explained: "If I, your Lord and Teacher, have washed your feet, you also ought to wash one another's feet. For I have given you an example, that you also should do just as I have done for you" (John 13:14-15). Showing love means putting others before ourselves, even if it means getting our hands dirty.

A good indication that a character is becoming a "hero" is when she or he sets aside personal desires for someone else's good. How much are you willing to give for others? Jesus said His disciples should be known by their "love." Our reputation as Christians is built on giving ourselves away for others. As God leads you on your own hero's journey, don't be surprised if He gives you opportunities to serve others. It is in those moments that you truly become heroic.

DISCOVER

In what ways does our culture encourage us to be selfish rather than selfless?

Serving others can take many different forms, not just washing feet! List several ways you can serve people in your life this week.

ACT

Look for an opportunity to serve someone else in a practical way today. Let this prayer guide you: *Lord, thank You for loving me enough to sacrifice everything for me. Help me serve others today in a way that reflects the example You gave. Amen.*

Day 34

SEEING REALITY

Do not be conformed to this age, but be transformed by
the renewing of your mind, so that you may discern what is
the good, pleasing, and perfect will of God.
— Romans 12:2

EXPLORE

many narratives have played around with the idea of true versus false perception. In the science-fiction novel *Ready Player One*, characters can access an immersive virtual reality universe called the Oasis. By entering an "immersion rig" and wearing virtual reality goggles, they can experience an exciting virtual existence, changing their appearance, developing in-world relationships, and constructing an entirely new life story. The experience is so engrossing that some players lose their grasp on reality, remaining in the Oasis while their bodies starve to death or choosing to stay in the Oasis until they can no longer distinguish between their real selves and their avatars.[10]

People sometimes believe Christianity is primarily about actions. When we talk about becoming more like Christ, we may think almost exclusively in terms of changing our behavior to do things Jesus would do and not do things that would displease Him. Your actions should reflect Jesus, but He also desires to transform how you think and see the world. After all, your thoughts impact your behavior. You must see the world as Jesus does before you can act like Him.

It's not that Christians should only think about religious topics or exclusively watch faith-based movies or just listen to worship songs. Rather, everything we see, hear, or do should be filtered through the lens of faith. One

GOD, HEROES, AND EVERYDAY DRAGONS

of the primary character arcs in your faith journey will be the transformation of your perspective as you come to see the world as Jesus sees it. The lens through which we perceive the world is often referred to as our "worldview"— a religion or belief system that colors what we see. The question is, what worldview glasses are you wearing?

> You must see the
> world as Jesus
> does before you
> can act like Him.

Jesus describes Satan as the "father of lies" (see John 8:44). One of the devil's favorite tools is constructing a skewed reality—a tainted pair of glasses—and then watching us live in it. In contrast, Jesus declared that He is the Truth (see John 14:6). To maintain our grip on reality, we must allow Him to "transform" and "renew" our minds (see Rom. 12:2). As God changes your thoughts, you'll see the world around you more clearly, distinguishing truth from falsehood and discerning "what is the good, pleasing, and perfect will of God" (12:2).

Rather than judging people, you will see them as sinners in need of salvation. You will no longer view others as a means to an end but as people you can serve. You won't lose hope when the journey becomes hard, because you'll know God is with you. You won't accept the world's lies that you're worthless, because you'll see yourself as a priceless creation whom God loves.

The hero's journey is not just about what you do but about who you become. It's about God fundamentally transforming your mind so you think and see the world as He does. After all, a hero who cannot distinguish between good and evil isn't much of a hero. As you travel, look through the lens of Jesus so you clearly see God's good and pleasing truth for your life.

DISCOVER

In what ways do you see the world differently than your non-Christian friends do? Write down three examples.

List an area of your life where you think God wants to change your thinking. Why does God want to change it?

ACT

Let this prayer guide you today: *Lord, please help me see the world in light of who You are and what You have done through Jesus. Please change any areas of my thinking that are misaligned with Your good, pleasing, and perfect will. Amen.*

Day 35

CHARACTER TRAITS

But the fruit of the Spirit is love, joy, peace, patience,
kindness, goodness, faithfulness, gentleness, and
self-control. The law is not against such things.
— Galatians 5:22-23

EXPLORE

Characterization is an essential part of any good story. We call characters who lack interesting traits "flat." In video games such as the *Elder Scrolls* or *Fallout* series, players begin by creating an avatar. The process is not just about choosing the appearance but also about constructing a personality. Players adjust strengths and weaknesses, select skills, and choose a play type (a brute warrior or a stealthy thief?). Usually, these traits develop and change over the course of the game.

As a character in God's story, you have personality traits too. You were born with some, and you accumulated others along the way. God's creativity is infinite. No two of His characters are the same. Each has unique quirks and traits.

Yet, the Bible provides a list of features that should describe all Christians. The apostle Paul calls these features the "fruit of the Spirit" (Gal. 5:22-23). The Holy Spirit will develop these character traits in your life along the journey, like fruit on a tree. Fruit takes time to develop and must be nurtured to reach maturity. Once the fruit has grown, it is visible to others. In fact, looking at the fruit is the easiest way to identify the tree type.

Read the "fruit" listed in Galatians 5:22-23. Even if some of these traits come more naturally to you than others, they aren't all present in your life to the degree God desires. You will experience a "character arc" as God develops these attributes in you.

What is the result? Interestingly, fruit doesn't immediately benefit the tree. A tree doesn't gain any energy from the fruit. In fact, growing fruit costs the tree something. The process by which God instills these good character traits in us may not be easy (has learning patience ever been a pleasant experience?). Rather, fruit benefits those outside the tree. When we buy fresh produce from the grocery store, we reap the reward of the tree's effort. As the Holy Spirit develops holy characteristics and fruit in us, others are blessed.

> As God grows and develops your character, the fruit of your life will point people to the God who is at work in you.

Fruit also contains seeds. When those seeds are deposited on the ground, some take root and eventually become new trees. The character traits the Holy Spirit develops in you may also become the seeds that result in other people's salvation. As God grows and develops your character, the fruit of your life will point people to the God who is at work in you (see 2 Thess. 1:11-12).

What will your character arc be? What traits and characteristics need to grow in your life to shape you into the person God has called you to be? Don't lose heart if you are weak in some areas. Growth is an exciting opportunity. Be patient, trust in God's power and wisdom, and watch as He grows your heroic character.

DISCOVER

Of the "fruit of the Spirit" listed in Galatians 5:22-23, which ones do you most need to grow?

_____

_____

_____

_____

_____

In what ways can our positive characteristics point people to Jesus? When people praise us for our "goodness," how can we point them to God?

_____

_____

_____

_____

_____

ACT

Let this prayer guide you today: _Lord, thank You for the gift of the Holy Spirit. Please produce in my life the fruit of love, joy, peace, patience, kindness, goodness, faithfulness, gentleness, and self-control. Amen._

Day 36

WAY STATION

PART 5:
CHARACTER ARC

Identify the characteristics below as either a Strength (S) or Growth Area (GA). Next, rate the traits on a scale of -5 to +5 based on how evident they currently are in your life:

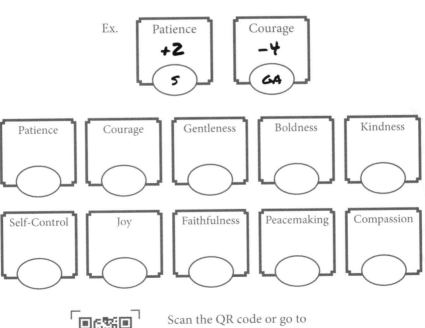

Ex.

Patience	Courage
+2	**-4**
S	GA

Patience	Courage	Gentleness	Boldness	Kindness

Self-Control	Joy	Faithfulness	Peacemaking	Compassion

Scan the QR code or go to lifeway.com/godheroesdragons to watch the video for Part 5: Character Arc.

PART 6:

CROSSING THE THRESHOLD

Day 37

KEEP MOVING FORWARD

Brothers and sisters, I do not consider myself to have taken hold of it. But one thing I do: Forgetting what is behind and reaching forward to what is ahead, I pursue as my goal the prize promised by God's heavenly call in Christ Jesus.
— Philippians 3:13-14

EXPLORE

*P*ilgrim's Progress, by John Bunyan, is one of the best-selling books of all time.[1] It's an allegory that imagines the Christian life as a fictional journey. "Christian," the protagonist, makes the difficult pilgrimage to the Celestial City, overcoming numerous obstacles along the way. At the beginning of the adventure, a character named Pliable joins Christian as a fellow traveler. At first, Pliable is a suitable companion, filled with good intentions of reaching the destination. But as the journey continues and trials intensify, his commitment is shaken. Eventually, at Slough of Despond—a deep, hopeless bog—Pliable quits. The journey proved too demanding for him.[2]

In every hero's journey, the protagonist must make important decisions. These pivotal moments are called "crossing the threshold."[3] Will the hero continue or turn back? Will he engage the threat or lose courage? Will she maintain commitment to the rebellion, even in the face of great personal sacrifice? These moments are like the "checkpoints" in video games, representing that one section of the adventure is complete, and another more difficult one is about to begin.

The Bible is filled with these moments. When the religious authorities threatened Peter and John and told them to stop talking about Jesus, the disciples boldly refused (see Acts 4:19-20). Ruth's mother-in-law tried to convince Ruth not to follow her, but Ruth declared, "Don't plead with me to abandon you or to return and not follow you. For wherever you go, I will go. . . . your people will be my people, and your God will be my God" (Ruth 1:16). Later, her great-grandson David volunteered to fight the giant Goliath, though David wasn't even a soldier. Once he left the camp and stepped onto the battlefield, he had crossed the threshold (see 1 Sam. 17:40).

> Journeys aren't just about the decision to begin; they also require a daily commitment to continue.

Unfortunately, not every character chooses to cross. When a wealthy young man asked Jesus what was required for him to gain eternal life, Jesus told him to sell all his possessions, give the money to the poor, and follow Him (see Mark 10:21). Unfortunately, the man was unwilling, so he turned away in disappointment.

As you travel on your faith journey, you will face thresholds. If you accept God's call to follow Him, your commitment will inevitably be tested. Journeys aren't just about the decision to begin; they also require a daily commitment to continue. The world is always calling you to wander off the path, turn back, or to quit and say, "I think I've come far enough." Thresholds are the moments when we decide to persevere.

How can you prepare for these big "threshold" moments? By trusting God each step of the way. David didn't start by fighting Goliath. When King Saul doubted David's ability, David recounted the times as a shepherd when he chased down and killed a lion or bear to rescue his sheep. Then he confidently claimed, "The LORD who rescued me from the paw of the lion and the paw of the bear will rescue me from the hand of this Philistine" (1 Sam. 17:37). Be faithful to trust and follow God step by step and, like David, you'll find you have the courage to cross bigger "thresholds" when they appear.

DISCOVER

Describe a moment in your life when you took a significant step of commitment in your faith journey.

When is it most difficult to stay committed to Jesus? What are some ways you have been encouraged to keep moving forward during those difficult times?

ACT

Pray this prayer of commitment today (only if you mean it): *Lord, today I commit myself again to pick up my cross and follow You. Please give me the strength I need to keep moving forward each day until I reach the end of the journey You have laid out for me. Amen.*

Day 38

TO THE END OF YOURSELF
AND BEYOND

*Then Jesus rebuked the demon, and it came out of him,
and from that moment the boy was healed. Then the
disciples approached Jesus privately and said, "Why couldn't
we drive it out?" "Because of your little faith," he told
them. "For truly I tell you, if you have faith the size of
a mustard seed, you will tell this mountain, 'Move from here
to there,' and it will move. Nothing will be impossible for you."
— Matthew 17:18-20*

Explore

In *The Wizard of Oz*, Dorothy meets three companions on her journey to the Emerald City: Scarecrow, Tin Man, and Lion. Each believes he lacks something important—a brain, a heart, and courage, respectively. They accompany Dorothy down the yellow brick road to ask the Wizard to give them what they lack. At various stages along the journey, they face obstacles that test their perceived weaknesses, but their love for Dorothy leads them to face the challenges head on. When they finally reach the Wizard, he tells them they already have what they seek. What they hoped to obtain at the end of the journey, they gained through the journey itself.[4]

A "threshold" represents the outer limit of what we think we can handle. A hero's path is often blocked

If you only do what you can handle alone, then you will never experience what only God can do.

118

by obstacles or "threshold guardians." [5] Crossing these thresholds is typically less about the size of the challenge itself and more about what the hero can handle. Thresholds represent moments when heroes seem to reach the limit of what they can overcome, but they must keep moving forward anyway.

A story in the Bible describes a time when the twelve disciples reached one of these thresholds. With God's power, they had been healing the sick, casting out demons, and performing many other miracles. It probably seemed like they could do anything! Then a father brought a demon-possessed boy to them that was beyond anything they had encountered before, and they failed. The disciples had cast out demons before, but this one was more powerful than they had ever faced. Thankfully, Jesus stepped in and healed the boy.

When the disciples asked why they failed, Jesus answered, "Because of your little faith." He explained that even with a faith the size of a tiny mustard seed, "nothing [would] be impossible" for them (see Matt. 17:14-20). The problem wasn't that they didn't have enough power at their disposal. They had all the strength they needed. They lacked faith. While the demon represented the immediate challenge, the true obstacle was internal. They had reached the end of what they believed they could handle, but to achieve victory—and set a young boy free—they needed to go deeper.

As you travel along your faith journey, God will take you to the end of what you think you can handle and then ask you to follow Him further. We can only experience what lies on the other side of the threshold by crossing it. The Bible says God can do "above and beyond all that we ask or think according to the power that works in us" (Eph. 3:20). There is no limit to what God can do in and through your life, and He loves you too much to leave you where you are. He will lead you to thresholds and beyond because other people will benefit from your faith. If you only do what you can handle alone, then you will never experience what only God can do.

DISCOVER

Are there things you believe you could never do? What is it about those things that makes them seem impossible?

_____

_____

_____

_____

_____

Have you ever done something you thought you couldn't do, only to discover that it wasn't nearly as difficult as you imagined? In what ways does reaching a "threshold" cause you to trust God in a deeper and more personal way?

_____

_____

_____

_____

ACT

Think of areas in your life where you need to do things that scare you or that seem impossible. Write down whatever comes to mind. Then take a few minutes to pray and ask God to grow your faith to do things that seem impossible.

Day 39

ACTIONS AND WORDS

*But someone will say, "You have faith, and
I have works." Show me your faith without
works, and I will show you faith by my works.*
— James 2:18

EXPLORE

I t's easier to tell stories about heroism than to live heroically. Surrounded by friends in a cozy inn, aspiring heroes may declare their willingness to slay dragons. But when they find themselves standing at the entrance to the dragon's lair, the true dragon slayers are separated from the pretenders.

One of the most significant thresholds we must cross on our hero's journey is putting our words into action. Peter was the most outspoken disciple. When he was surrounded by his friends, he boldly declared his unwavering allegiance to Jesus (see Matt. 26:33). Yet when Jesus was arrested and a servant girl recognized Peter as a disciple, Peter denied even knowing his teacher (see Matt. 26:69-70). The problem wasn't that Peter didn't sincerely believe what he said. Rather, he learned the painful lesson that it's easier to say something than to do it.

Jesus warned that not everyone who called Him Lord would enter His kingdom (see Matt. 7:21). It's easy to understand that people living in rebellion against God won't enter heaven, but it's more shocking that some who loudly proclaim Jesus as Lord won't either. Jesus was saying that some people who call Him Lord never cross the threshold of putting their professed belief into action.

To be clear, Christianity isn't about earning a ticket to heaven by accomplishing enough valiant deeds. Rather, actions reveal the truth about your belief. A faith journey is not merely something that happens in your head. In the Bible, James declared that his faith was evident by his actions (see James 2:18). If your faith is real, then it will be confirmed by your behavior. Actions takes faith—which is invisible—and makes it visible.

In *Harry Potter and the Chamber of Secrets*, the arrogant author Gilderoy Lockhart is hired as the new Defense Against the Dark Arts teacher. Lockhart is famous in the magical world for heroically defeating dangerous foes, and he is tasked with teaching the Hogwarts students to do likewise. But when evil forces infiltrate the school, he frantically packs his suitcase and prepares to flee. It turns out that Lockhart is a total fraud, and the famous stories he recounted in his books were fabricated or stolen. He had built his entire persona on being a champion against evil, but he ran away at the first opportunity to put his words to action.[6]

> If your faith is real, then it will be confirmed by your behavior. Actions takes faith—which is invisible—and makes it visible.

One of the most common reasons people outside the faith claim to have a negative opinion of Christianity is hypocrisy. They see Christians as people who talk a lot about what they believe (and tell others what to do or think) but are unwilling to put their faith into action.

What does your behavior reveal about what you believe? Are you willing to put your faith into action?

DISCOVER

In what areas have Christians been criticized for being
hypocrites? How does this discrepancy between words and
actions give the world a false picture of who Jesus is?

Think back over the last week or two. What evidence was there
in your life that you truly believe what you say you do? If you have
trouble thinking of anything, what actions can you take this week
to put your faith to work?

ACT

Pray this prayer throughout the day: *God, please guard my heart from
hypocrisy. Help me to act in a way that is consistent with my faith so my actions
point other people to You. Amen.*

Day 40

WALK BY FAITH

For we walk by faith, not by sight.
— 2 Corinthians 5:7

EXPLORE

During the climactic ending of *Star Wars: A New Hope*, Luke Skywalker flies his X-Wing starfighter down the trench of the dreaded Death Star. He has just one shot to hit a small exhaust opening with his proton torpedo. If he succeeds, the planet-destroying space station goes BOOM. If he misses, it's game over for the good guys. As he approaches the crucial moment, he does the unthinkable: he turns off his targeting computer. He's going to make the shot blind, or at least that's how it appears to the suddenly alarmed people back on the Rebel base. But audiences know he's not truly blind.[7]

When you clearly sense God is leading you to do something, obey Him, even if you don't see the full picture yet.

You may have heard people speak about Christianity as "blind faith." After all, if walking by faith means not walking by sight, as 2 Corinthians 5:7 indicates, then it seems believers are left to navigate blind. Yet, the Christian faith is never really blind. Faith is built on something. Otherwise, there would be no reason to follow one religion over any other. Walking by faith means trusting in a real God and allowing Him to guide you rather than attempting to navigate circumstances on your own.

Faith is trusting what you do know in the face of what you don't know. In the beginning of *A New*

Hope, Luke Skywalker is not yet the powerful Jedi he will become. There is much he still must learn. In an interesting moment that foreshadows Luke's later mission, Obi-Wan has Luke practice blocking laser bolts while his eyes are completely covered by a face shield, forcing him to rely only on "feeling" the Force. By the time he's flying down that Death Star trench, he has had enough experience with the Force to know he could trust it in a high-stakes situation.

To people who haven't experienced God's presence in their life, walking by faith might appear reckless. God doesn't usually answer our questions with a detailed "how to" instruction manual. Instead, our trust is built on a relationship with God. Many others throughout history have experienced God's love, power, and provision, and we can too.

We shouldn't abandon all rational thought and live our lives based wholly on emotions or feelings. As we explored in Part 4, "Companions & Guides," God has provided us the means of hearing and understanding His guidance. When you clearly sense God is leading you to do something, obey Him, even if you don't see the full picture yet.

Walking by faith rather than by sight isn't primarily about what you lose, that is, your own sight, but about what you gain—God's perspective on your circumstances. Walking by faith means trusting God as the final authority on your situation. God has a wider perspective than we do. When you learn to put your faith in Him and not limit yourself to your own narrow viewpoint, He will lead you to places you could never have imagined. Remember, it's a walk, not a run. Keep trusting Him one step at a time. Keep walking with Him.

DISCOVER

Why is "walking by faith, not by sight" so hard? Why doesn't God make it easier? What value is there in living this way?

Why did you become a Christian? What have you learned or experienced in the past that gives you confidence to trust God today and in the future?

ACT

Do you have to make a big decision soon? Are you in the middle of a confusing situation? Have you prayed and asked God for His perspective? Pray right now and ask God to help you walk forward according to His best wisdom.

Day 41

DOUBT

*Immediately Jesus reached out his hand, caught hold of him, and
said to him, "You of little faith, why did you doubt?"*
— *Matthew 14:31*

EXPLORE

Christopher Nolan's *Dark Knight* film trilogy is considered one of the greatest comic-book-to-film series ever made. In the final movie, *The Dark Knight Rises*, Bruce Wayne is trapped in a deep pit that serves as an underground prison. He is helpless as the villains wreak havoc in Gotham City. His only hope for escape is to climb the walls and make a seemingly impossible leap across a gap. With a rope attached for safety, he attempts the feat several times but fails. Eventually, a wise mentor challenges him to make the leap without a rope. Failure would mean certain death (and a really short Batman movie). He successfully makes the jump, escapes the prison, and saves his city.[8]

This thrilling scene underscores two truths about doubt. First, doubt can hold us back from reaching our true potential. Second, doubt is an inevitable experience in even the mightiest hero's journey.

Today's key verse, Matthew 14:31, is part of the famous story where Peter walked on the water toward Jesus. Notice the point in the story when Peter experienced uncertainty. We might have expected him to feel doubt while standing on the boat waiting to jump into the sea. After all, other than Jesus, no person in history had ever walked on water. Peter had faith to attempt the impossible. Then, in the middle of the miracle, he felt the "strength of the wind" (v. 30), and he doubted. Often, we read this passage as a story of Peter's failure. It's true that the other disciples didn't doubt or sink into the sea—but it's because they never left the boat! Peter's doubts were the result of following Jesus to a place well beyond his own abilities.

Perhaps you've been taught that doubts are sinful or shameful. Yet even the mightiest Bible heroes had moments of doubt and uncertainty. In fact, if a Christian never feels doubts, then perhaps he or she has never followed Jesus to uncomfortable places.

> Constantly questioning everything and refusing to step forward until we have absolute certainty may truly be disobedience in disguise.

One of the most honest statements in the entire Bible comes from a man who declared to Jesus, "I do believe; help my unbelief!" (see Mark 9:24). Having faith doesn't mean knowing everything. Remember, yesterday we described faith as "trusting what you do know in the face of what you don't know." Whenever you face the unknown, you will experience doubts. The solution to these doubts is to trust what you do know—or more specifically, *who* you know.

There is a significant difference between honest doubts and continual skepticism. Doubts arise when we faithfully follow Jesus to difficult places. On the other hand, constantly questioning everything and refusing to step forward until we have absolute certainty may truly be disobedience in disguise. It's okay to be nervous; but at some point, Jesus will inevitably lead you to step out of your comfortable boat. Be encouraged, for that is when miracles happen.

DISCOVER

What is one part of your life where you experience doubt? What would give you more confidence in this area?

How can you find strength and courage to "step out of the boat," even when you're scared?

ACT

Do you have questions about faith or the Bible? Are there things you struggle to believe? We encourage you to take time to search for videos about "Christian apologetics" on the internet. There are a lot of good videos of great Christian communicators addressing some tricky questions. Don't worry if some of this stuff goes over your head. Click around and find videos that explain things in a way that makes sense to you.

Day 42

REST FOR THE JOURNEY AHEAD

"Come to me, all of you who are weary and burdened, and I will give you rest. Take my yoke upon you and learn from me, because I am lowly and humble in heart, and you will find rest for your souls. For my yoke is easy and my burden is light."
— Matthew 11:28-30

EXPLORE

Have you ever heard of a superhero taking a nap?

For a hero, resting is certainly less glamorous than fighting. Our ideal hero keeps fighting the good fight day after day with no need to rest. Yet even the mightiest heroes grow weary. In every Avengers movie, despite the Avengers being "Earth's mightiest heroes," the action slows down at some point and the heroes find refuge somewhere—Hawkeye's house on the farm, aboard Nick Fury's helicarrier, or at Avengers HQ—to rest and recharge before the next fight.

Rest is built into God's perfect design. The Bible reveals that even God, the only one who never gets tired, rested on the seventh day of creation as an example for us (see Gen. 2:2-3). Mimicking that pattern, He later established the Sabbath as a day for humans to rest. Before Jesus calmed the stormy sea in today's verse, the frightened disciples found Him sleeping below deck. After speaking to crowds all day under the hot Mediterranean sun, even Jesus, the Son of God, was taking a power nap! In fact, Jesus often went somewhere to recharge and connect with His Father.

> You will find rest by walking with Jesus, not charging ahead of Him.

Over the last few days, we've explored why heroes must keep moving forward. The hero's journey is a journey, after all. The hero will never find success by standing still. But the quest can't be completed in a day. The hero's journey is more of a marathon than a sprint. The hero must know when to keep pushing forward and when to stop and camp for the night.

Jesus promises you rest (see Matt. 11:28). But it's important to clarify that "rest" is not the same as "sleep." The rest Jesus described is perhaps better thought of as refreshment, like an ice-cold Gatorade and a warm shower after a workout.

Resting doesn't mean quitting or forgetting the mission. Jesus instructed His followers: "Take my yoke" (Matt. 11:29). A yoke is the piece of equipment that connected two oxen to a farming wagon. Essentially, Jesus was saying to let Him do the heavy lifting for a while so you can recharge for the work ahead. Jesus was describing deeper rest than vegging while binge-watching Netflix for hours. As C. S. Lewis put it, "Our Father refreshes us on the journey with some pleasant inns, but will not encourage us to mistake them for home."[9]

Don't neglect rest. It's true: we don't sing epic songs about noble heroes who sprinted from the village on a quest only to pass out on the side of the road a few miles later. But the journey is long and difficult. Fortunately, you don't travel alone. You will find rest by walking with Jesus, not charging ahead of Him.

DISCOVER

Excluding sleep, what activity is most restful for you? What drains your energy?

_____

_____

_____

_____

Do you practice a "Sabbath" during your week when you take time to rest and refocus on God through worship? Why or why not?

_____

_____

_____

_____

ACT

Intentionally take a Sabbath day of rest this week. Set aside work, but don't waste the day being lazy. "Vegging" is not necessarily the same as resting. Instead, focus on God, not just by attending a church service but by making space in your day for prayer, Bible reading, and sitting in silence before God. Take a walk outside in God's creation, and pray as you go. Did God speak to you as you walked, prayed, and listened? Did you feel rested after your Sabbath?

Day 43

WAY STATION

PART 6:
CROSSING THE THRESHOLD

What are your thresholds? Write down three current fears and three doubts you have about where God might lead you on your hero's journey.

Fears:	Doubts:
1.	1.
2.	2.
3.	3.

Scan the QR code or go to lifeway.com/ godheroesdragons to watch the video for Part 6: Crossing the Threshold.

PART 7:
TRIALS & ADVERSITY

Day 44

CONFLICT

*Even when I go through the darkest valley, I fear no danger, for
you are with me; your rod and your staff — they comfort me.*
— Psalm 23:4

EXPLORE

ood stories require conflict. No one is interested in watching a movie about a superhero who simply goes about mundane daily activities— wakes up, checks social media, does a thousand push ups, drinks coffee, walks the dog, and so on. The hero must overcome adversity for the narrative to have a sense of importance, which is why many stories include a villain. But conflict doesn't always take the form of an antagonistic character. In natural disaster movies, the fight is between humanity and nature. In a drama, the problem may be a terminal illness. Sometimes the challenge is internal, with characters battling their own thoughts and emotions. Whatever form it takes, conflict is an essential part of good storytelling.

As you undertake your faith journey, you will experience adversity. The central conflict in God's story—sin—was set in motion from the beginning, but there are many other roadblocks that will be in your way. Jesus said His followers would face troubles (see John 15:18-19), and Paul wrote that "all who want

> If you continue your journey, you will experience obstacles. The good news is that you won't face them alone. The Spirit that gave Jesus victory over death goes with you now.

to live a godly life in Christ Jesus will be persecuted" (2 Tim. 3:12). Conflict is coming. The question is, how will you confront it?

In the Old Testament, King David was no stranger to conflict. But regardless of his circumstances, he had confidence that God was with him. In one of David's most famous psalms, he declared, "Even though I walk through the valley of the shadow of death, I will fear no evil, for you are with me; your rod and your staff, they comfort me" (Ps. 23:4 ESV). If you are near enough to death to be in its "shadow," your situation is dire!

When writing about the hero's journey, Joseph Campbell often referred to the conflict the hero encounters as "the Shadow." [1] One of the earliest and most universal childhood fears is of the dark. Shadows are intimidating because darkness hides our view of what lies ahead. The best horror movies merely hint at showing the monster, revealing it fully only near the end. In the shadows, our imaginations convince us we're doomed.

A situation may seem hopeless—until somebody turns on a light. The disciple John, referring to Jesus, said, "[the] light shines in the darkness, and yet the darkness did not overcome it" (John 1:5). Your journey may be difficult; there will be battles to fight and valleys to cross. But the victor has already been decided. Jesus didn't just walk through the "shadow" of death. He faced death head on—and won. Because of Jesus, the apostle Paul confidently declared, "Death has been swallowed up in victory. Where, death, is your victory? Where, death, is your sting?" (1 Cor. 15:55). That same hope lives in you.

If you continue your journey, you will experience obstacles. The good news is that you won't face them alone. The Spirit that gave Jesus victory over death goes with you now. If God has defeated death, then He can empower you to face any challenge that lies ahead. Press on, fight the good fight, and take comfort that the Light of the world goes with you, and the darkness—no matter how frightening—will never overcome Him.

DISCOVER

What are some of your biggest fears? How does Jesus's power and victory over sin and death give you hope to face these fears head on?

What areas of the world around you appear filled with darkness right now? How can God shine His light through you into these areas?

ACT

Think of any conflict or opposition you are currently experiencing. Take a minute now to pray and give your fears, frustrations, and questions to God. Ask for His strength and wisdom to be victorious in the way He desires you to be.

Day 45

ARMOR

Finally, be strengthened by the Lord and by his vast strength. Put on the full armor of God so that you can stand against the schemes of the devil.
— Ephesians 6:10-11

EXPLORE

In the video game *The Legend of Zelda*, players begin outside a cave in an expansive open world. Inside the cave is an old man who famously declares, "It's dangerous to go alone! Take this," before giving the player a sword. The cave contains an essential item, but entering is optional.[2] However, players who rush off on their adventure without going into the cave and getting the sword typically don't last long! While it may be tempting to charge ahead, proper preparation is important.

Before your go any further, read Ephesians 6:10-20. In the book of Ephesians, the apostle Paul was writing to one of the first churches. The Christian movement was young and would face great opposition in the days ahead. In fact, Paul wrote these words from inside a prison cell. He instructed the church to prepare for their journey by putting on "the armor of God" (see Eph. 6:11). Paul's readers would have been familiar with armor, because they saw it all the time on Roman soldiers. But the armor Paul instructed them to put on was completely different.

Notice that the armor is not designed to protect against earthly enemies but against spiritual powers. As a Christian, your strength to face spiritual opposition doesn't stem from your own abilities but from "the Lord and by his vast strength" (Eph. 6:10). The further you go on your faith journey, the more likely you are to become a target for spiritual forces bent on challenging God and His Kingdom. If evil powers oppose God and you have given your life to Jesus as Lord, then you've declared your allegiance to Him. You are no longer neutral in the spiritual war.

The battle between Jesus and the devil has already been decided. Paul said, "[God] disarmed the rulers and authorities and disgraced them publicly; he triumphed over them in [Jesus]" (Col. 2:15). Jesus has already been victorious in that fight! However, we are still engaged in the battle. Thankfully, God has given us every tool we need to win. Are you experiencing the "flaming arrows of the evil one" (Eph. 6:16)? God has given you the shield of faith to extinguish those. Lean into your faith and God's promises, and you will not fall captive to the lies of the devil.

> The further you go on your faith journey, the more likely you are to become a target for spiritual forces bent on challenging God and His Kingdom.

The devil is like a lion, prowling around looking for someone to devour (see 1 Peter 5:8). How should we respond? The Bible says to resist him (see 1 Peter 5:9; James 4:7) and he will flee. In *The Pilgrim's Progress* (remember, this story is an allegory for Christianity), the protagonist, Christian, walks up the path to a rest stop on his journey but notices two fearsome lions on either side of the door. Terrified, he is about to turn back when someone calls to him from the house, "Fear not the lions, for they are chained . . . Keep in the midst of the path, and no hurt shall come to thee." [3] In his fear, Christian had not noticed that the lions were chained to the wall. He would be safe if he stuck to the path.

The same is true for you. Don't fear the "lions" on your journey, for God has equipped you with everything you need for victory. Suit up, stay on the path, and move forward in confidence.

DISCOVER

In your life, what "warning signs" indicate you're veering off the right path?

_____

_____

_____

_____

_____

_____

_____

ACT

There is a scene in many classic action movies in which the heroes "suit up." It's usually edited into an epic montage scored with a killer soundtrack. Consider this your "suiting up" montage. In the verses you read today, Paul names several elements included with the armor of God. Take a moment to pray through each item on the list below and ask God to equip you for the day ahead (see Eph. 6:12-17 NIV).

- The "belt of truth" (v. 14)
- The "breastplate of righteousness" (v. 14)
- Feet fitted with the readiness of the "gospel of peace" (v. 15)
- The "shield of faith" (v. 16)
- The "helmet of salvation" (v. 17)
- The "sword of the Spirit" (v. 17)

Day 46

HATED BY THE WORLD

"If you were of the world, the world would love you as its own. However, because you are not of the world, but I have chosen you out of it, the world hates you."
— John 15:19

EXPLORE

Perhaps no element of storytelling is more pervasive than the conflict between heroes and villains. A couple of mean stepsisters try to prevent Cinderella from finding happiness; Moriarty seeks to outwit Sherlock Holmes; Rey and Kylo Ren must face off to determine the fate of the galaxy. Even many of the most popular video games, from *Super Smash Bros.* to *Fortnite,* are designed to let players battle it out to be the last one standing.

You may not be surrounded by dark lords and supervillains, but today's culture often operates the same way. It encourages an "us versus them" mindset. When people hold different views on political or social issues, they are pitted against each other as "enemies." We are urged to "play to win" and to crush the opposition into submission.

The pressure intensifies when you become a Christian. As a Christian, you are spiritually alive in a spiritually dead world (see Eph. 2:2). You are fundamentally different from the people around you. Jesus said the world would hate His followers (see John 15:19). If you are a Christian, you should expect to encounter hostility.

Even in the face of resistance, Jesus instructed His followers to do the unexpected: "You have heard that it was said, Love your neighbor and hate your enemy. But I tell you, love your enemies and pray for those who persecute

> God calls Christians to rise above the conflict and do the unthinkable: answer hate with love.

you" (Matt. 5:43-44). The world says to fight "fire with fire," but Jesus commanded us to fight fire with water. The apostle Paul confidently declared, "For though we live in the world, we do not wage war as the world does. The weapons we fight with are not the weapons of the world. On the contrary, they have divine power to demolish strongholds" (2 Cor. 10:3-4 NIV). Christians will experience opposition, but we shouldn't respond the way the world does.

Jesus set the example for us to follow. He boldly confronted sin, but He loved people, even when no one else did. He didn't wage war against people but for them. He didn't act out of spiteful retaliation or to "win" the conflict but to combat the sin that prevented people from fully experiencing God's love. Jesus's example had a major effect on the apostle Paul. He actively hunted down and imprisoned Christians until He met Jesus. After that life-changing encounter, he encouraged the very people he once persecuted, "Do not be conquered by evil, but conquer evil with good" (Rom. 12:21).

Have you ever been treated differently because you're a Christian? Have people ever mocked you for your faith? Perhaps you've inadvertently become the center of attention for not indulging in the same sinful activities as the people around you. Let's face it: nobody likes to be hated, bullied, or ridiculed. It can be tempting to hide our faith or to retaliate in anger. But God calls Christians to rise above the conflict and do the unthinkable: answer hate with love.

Ultimately, God wants the world to know Jesus. God hasn't called you to defeat or destroy sinners. Vengeance is His job, not yours (see Rom. 12:19). Your mission is to show people a better way through your words and actions. By doing the unexpected and loving even those who hate you, God may use you to turn enemies into allies.

DISCOVER

Is there anyone in your life right now whom you might consider an enemy? How can you respond to that person in love instead of hate?

In what ways does our culture urge us to view others with hate or disgust? How can we avoid falling into this trap?

ACT

Take sixty seconds to pray specifically for the person you named above as an enemy. Throughout your day, continue to bring that person before God in prayer. Try to make this practice an ongoing habit. Write down what you see God do in that person's (and your) life.

Day 47

AT WAR WITH SELF

For I do not do the good that I want to do, but I practice the evil that I do not want to do. Now if I do what I do not want, I am no longer the one that does it, but it is the sin that lives in me. — Romans 7:19-20

EXPLORE

Anti-heroes have become increasingly popular in modern stories. While noble and virtuous protagonists like Superman or Wonder Woman are admirable, audiences are often captivated by flawed or conflicted heroes. Characters like Batman and Wolverine are interesting because of the internal battles that rage within them. They are good guys, but they struggle not to become like their enemies. They want to do good, but they constantly combat their weaknesses.

When describing the hero's journey, Joseph Campbell refers to the hero's opposition as the "Shadow," because the conflict often reflects the hero.[4] Even when adversity takes the form of a villain, the antagonist is usually a twisted version of the hero, hence the classic villainous line, "We're not so different, you and I!" Many early Marvel villains were evil copies of the hero, with similar powers and abilities but without the noble spirit. Even when battling enemies, the greatest conflict is often the one raging within the hero's own heart and mind.

> Only Jesus has completed the hero's journey as a true, perfect hero. The rest of us are anti-heroes, flawed and sinful but on a mission to follow Jesus.

144

The apostle Paul understood the raging that goes on inside each of us. He knew that although he was saved from the ultimate consequences of sin, he continued to experienced temptation: "For I do not do the good that I want to do, but I practice the evil that I do not want to do" (Rom. 7:19). Have you ever been in that situation? You had good intentions and knew what the Bible teaches. But in the heat of the moment, you found yourself doing the exact opposite of what you should.

One of the most disappointing experiences is knowing you underperformed. As an athlete, it's always painful to lose, but it's even worse when you know you could have played better. Making poor life choices is bad, but giving into sin as a Christian is especially discouraging. In the aftermath of failure, some Christians quit the journey, feeling unworthy to travel with a perfect hero like Jesus. Have you ever felt that way?

Perhaps the most challenging opponent you will face as a Christian is yourself. It is impossible to hide from ourselves. Jesus called Satan the "father of lies" (see John 8:44). Guilt and self-doubt are some of Satan's most deadly weapons. How can we combat this challenge?

We should begin by humbly acknowledging our imperfection. The difference between an anti-hero and a villain is intention. Both feel the pull toward evil, but the hero resists. Christians battle the same sinful nature as everyone else. But by choosing to follow Jesus, you become part of God's family. Jesus said, "I give them eternal life, and they will never perish. No one will snatch them out of my hand. My Father, who has given them to me, is greater than all" (John 10:28-29).

Only Jesus has completed the hero's journey as a true, perfect hero. The rest of us are anti-heroes, flawed and sinful but on a mission to follow Jesus. Your worthiness doesn't depend on you but on Jesus. When you stumble and fall, know that one day God will give you the ultimate and eternal victory.

DISCOVER

What lies have crept into your mind? What does the Bible say about these thoughts?

Emotions are important, but they can easily be misguided. How can we determine if our emotions are based on truth?

ACT

Pray this prayer today: *God, please help me to anchor my thoughts on truth today. When I am in danger of believing lies, bring Scripture to my mind to clarify my situation. Amen.*

Day 48

NEVER ALONE

"And remember, I am with you always, to the end of the age."
— Matthew 28:20b

EXPLORE

Brave heroes, exhausted from their valiant fight, stand with their backs against the wall as enemy hordes close in around them. This scene unfolds in countless tales. Can you think of a single story in which the good guys outnumbered their enemies? A classic storytelling trope is that evil finds its power in numbers. Unrelenting waves of enemy soldiers crashing against the hero forms the basis of many plots, including zombie apocalypse and alien invasion movies.

Over the last few days, we've explored various obstacles you will encounter on your journey. But sometimes the most difficult aspect of the conflict is not the challenge itself but the relentlessness of the attack. When every day brings a new trial, it can be exhausting to stay on your feet. Do you ever feel overwhelmed? Does life sometimes feel too difficult to face on your own? Here's the good news: You're never alone, and you have the upper hand in any battle.

There's a story in the Old Testament in which the prophet Elisha and his servant are surrounded by a large enemy army bent on capturing them. The servant is overwhelmed, but Elisha comforts him: "'Don't be afraid, for those who are with us outnumber those who are with them.' Then Elisha prayed, 'LORD, please open his eyes and let him see.' So the LORD opened the servant's eyes, and he saw that the mountain was covered with horses and chariots of fire all around Elisha" (2 Kings 6:16-17). It's like the scene in *The Lord of the*

Rings: The Return of the King when the invisible Army of the Dead appears to turn what looked like defeat into a rout for the good guys.[5]

When God is involved, the scales of any conflict are always decisively weighed in a Christian's favor. Right before Jesus left His disciples to return to heaven, He promised, "I am with you always, to the end of the age" (Matt. 28:20). They would not see Him again in a physical form, but Jesus said they had Someone even better: the Spirit of God dwelling within them (see John 14:16-17). No force on earth could remove the Spirit from them. The disciples couldn't see God's presence among them in the same way they could see Jesus's physical body, but they soon learned to trust His power. They courageously defied the powerful Roman Empire and the religious authorities because they knew they didn't stand alone.

> When you feel overwhelmed or anxious that the conflict is too big to handle, fix your eyes on the truth that you are never alone.

As a Christian, that power dwells in you. When you feel overwhelmed or anxious that the conflict is too big to handle, fix your eyes on the truth that you are never alone. When you feel lonely, dwell in God's presence. When you become overwhelmed, trust in God's power. When you are confused, rely on God's guidance. One of the most comforting truths of the Bible is that your journey is not a solo mission. God doesn't give you a backpack of supplies and wish you luck as you go. Instead, He walks with you every step of the way.

DISCOVER

When do you feel the most overwhelmed or lonely? How do you desire for God to make Himself known to you?

In what ways can you remind yourself that God is with you during your day?

ACT

It's wonderful to know we're never alone! But not everyone experiences that comfort. Is somebody in your life lonely? If you see someone sitting alone at school or on the bus or at church, here's a brave action you can take: go sit with that person. Just as God is with you, give that same assurance to someone else today. One simple gesture, like sitting with someone, can go a long way in battling loneliness.

Day 49

A CHANGE IN PERSPECTIVE

Count it all joy, my brothers, when you meet trials of various kinds, for you know that the testing of your faith produces steadfastness. And let steadfastness have its full effect, that you may be perfect and complete, lacking in nothing.
— James 1:2-4 (ESV)

EXPLORE

onflict is inevitable. What makes stories interesting is how characters deal with opposition or setbacks. The famous atheist philosopher Friedrich Nietzsche once wrote, "What does not destroy me, makes me stronger." [6] Sadly, this statement isn't always true. Simply experiencing trials doesn't necessarily turn someone into a hero. In fact, it can do the opposite.

The tragic loss of his parents eventually molds Bruce Wayne into the Dark Knight, a symbol of justice. His nemesis Harvey Dent (a.k.a. Two-Face) allows trials to transform him from Gotham's "White Knight" into a villain, prompting the famous quote, "You either die a hero or you live long enough to see yourself become the villain." [7] Dent was suggesting that the more challenges you face, the greater the likelihood that they will break you. Trials don't always make us stronger, but our response to them can.

We tend to think of challenges as bad. But according to James, Christians should "consider it a great joy" when we face trials (James 1:2). Just as athletes lift weights to strain and ultimately strengthen their muscles, God uses challenges to grow our faith.

Tests aren't always pleasant, but they reveal our strengths and weaknesses. You may ace some tests. Other times, you will barely scrape by or even fail. But

> On your own, trials can break you, but with God, these challenges are exciting opportunities to be further shaped into the hero that God has called you to be.

a failed test is not the end of the journey. In fact, it may become a significant learning moment. The best stories see the hero fail at least once before achieving the goal. This is part of the reason why *The Empire Strikes Back* is considered by many to be the greatest Star Wars movie in the franchise: Luke fails to defeat Darth Vader, and it makes Luke's victory in *Return of the Jedi* all the more sweet.[8]

God can use both victories and failures to grow the "steadfastness" of your faith. As Paul said in his letter to the Philippians, he was "sure of this, that he who started a good work in you will carry it on to completion until the day of Christ Jesus" (Phil. 2:6).

Everybody faces trials; but not everybody faces them the same way. Trust God when you encounter challenges. Be patient and preserve, knowing that in both exhilarating victories and demoralizing defeat, God will not let your efforts go to waste. On your own, trials can break you, but with God, these challenges are exciting opportunities for you to be further shaped into the hero that God has called you to be.

DISCOVER

Think of a test you failed (or on which you received a lower grade than you had hoped). How did you feel? How did you respond? Did you learn anything from the experience?

What does "steadfast" faith look like? Can you give some examples of this type of faith?

ACT

Let this prayer be on your mind throughout the day: *God, please prepare me for whatever tests of faith I face today. Continue to make me steadfast by helping me learn from both my victories and the times when I fail. Amen.*

Day 50

WAY STATION

PART 7:
TRIALS & ADVERSITY

Give the following "conflicts" a rating on a scale from 1 to 10 for how much you relate to them (1 being "not at all" and 10 being "completely"). Circle the highest-rated conflict in each grouping.

Ex.   Doubt **3**
Low Self-Esteem **7**
Loneliness **4**

Internal Conflict(s):

Doubt ____   Loneliness _____

Low self-esteem _____   Fear ____

External Conflict(s):

Unsupportive family ____   Relationships at church _____

Peer pressure from friends _____   Influence of Hollywood and media _____

Peer pressure from classmates _____

Scan the QR code or go to lifeway.com/godheroesdragons to watch the video for Part 7: Trials & Adversity.

PART 8:

THE
RETURN

Day 51

A PURPOSEFUL RETURN

"But you will receive power when the Holy Spirit has come on you, and you will be my witnesses in Jerusalem, in all Judea and Samaria, and to the ends of the earth."
— Acts 1:8

EXPLORE

D*on Quixote* is often considered the first modern novel ever written. It tells the story of a middle-aged nobleman who reads so many adventure stories that he loses his mind and sets off to become a knight, riding around the Spanish countryside looking for foes to battle and damsels to rescue. It's a comedy, because rather than helping people, Don Quixote is a burden to everyone around him. He's the hero nobody wants or needs.[1] The famous novel showcases the truth that it is not just adventure that makes a hero. Without a destination or purpose, a quest is just aimless wandering.

What sets people apart as heroes is not how they begin but how they return. What have they gained? Have they defeated the threat or accomplished their goal? Are they unchanged or unrecognizable? Christopher Vogler, who created a screenwriting textbook based on Joseph Campbell's work, called the final stage of the hero's journey the "Return with the Elixir."[2] This "elixir" can be anything heroes obtain that they can use to bless others.

What about you? Throughout your journey, God will lead you to overcome opposition, witness

Pass on what you have learned on your journey so others might experience the treasure you have found.

miracles, and travel further than you ever thought you could. What will you gain on the journey? Jesus said, "The kingdom of heaven is like treasure, buried in a field, that a man found and reburied. Then in his joy he goes and sells everything he has and buys that field" (Matt. 13:44). The treasure you acquire on your faith journey is no mere trinket.

An important element of the hero's journey is that the "elixir" doesn't only benefit the hero. An elixir is a magical potion or medicine; it has the power to heal, strengthen, or cleanse. A hero uses it to help others.

Acts 1:8 tell us that after journeying alongside the disciples for three years, Jesus sent them out to be His witnesses locally ("Jerusalem"), regionally ("Judea and Samaria"), and globally ("to the ends of the earth"). A whole new adventure awaited them. They had completed one journey, and they were ready to embark on a new one. Spreading the gospel around the world was too big of a task for a handful of fishermen, but the disciples were no longer the same people they were when they began. They had experienced God's power and would soon receive the gift of the Holy Spirit (see Acts 2:1-3).

You are part of their legacy. They were faithful to take the gospel to faraway places and to people who were different from them. Now it's your turn. Pass on what you have learned on your journey so others might experience the treasure you have found.

DISCOVER

What do you feel is your purpose? How does this purpose impact the way you act, spend time, and make decisions?

What changes has God made in your life since you decided to follow Jesus? In what ways can these changes be a blessing to others?

ACT

Think of someone you know who is not a Christian. Ask God to give you an opportunity to be a witness to them this week. Don't worry about what to say. Just be honest about what God has done in your life. This whole book is about stories. Share *your* story with someone else today.

Day 52

A HERO'S LEGACY

All these were approved through their faith, but they did not receive
what was promised, since God had provided something better for
us, so that they would not be made perfect without us. Therefore,
since we also have such a large cloud of witnesses surrounding us,
let us lay aside every hindrance and the sin that so easily ensnares
us. Let us run with endurance the race that lies before us.
— Hebrews 11:39–12:1

EXPLORE

When Rohan is on the verge of annihilation in *The Two Towers*, King Théoden declares, "If this is to be our end, then I would have them make such an end as to be worthy of remembrance!" [3] Heroes leave a legacy. Medieval heroes strove to inspire songs about their valiant deeds. Some were motivated by vanity. Those with nobler hearts wished to pass on a legacy that would inspire future generations.

In *Star Wars: The Force Awakens*, the little alien Maz Kanata tells the new heroes, "Through the ages, I've seen evil take many forms. The Sith. The Empire. Today, it is the First Order. Their shadow's spreading across the galaxy. We must face them. Fight them! All of us." [4] Every generation faces unique challenges, but heroes draw inspiration from those who have come before them.

Hebrews 11 is sometimes called the "Hall of Faith," since it lists many famous Bible heroes: Abel, Enoch, Noah, Abraham, Sarah, Isaac, Jacob, Joseph, Moses, Joshua, Rahab, Gideon, Barak, Samson, Jephthah, David, and Samuel. Other notable characters are hinted at but not named, such as Daniel and the trio of Shadrach, Meshach, and Abednego. How many of these names do you recognize?

You probably expected to see some of these names on this list, but others may have surprised you. Including a prostitute on a list of Bible heroes like Abraham and Jacob might be unexpected, but because of her faith, Rahab makes the cut. While some of these heroes are household names, you might not have any idea who Barak or Jephthah are! Nevertheless, they lived their faith journey in such a way that later generations honored them.

As great as these people are, the author of Hebrews wrote that something even greater awaited the Christians of his day (see Heb. 11:40). If we were to update the "Hall of Faith," to include New Testament heroes we would likely include names like Paul, Peter, Mary, Timothy, and Stephen. We might even add more recent champions like Corrie Ten Boom and C. S. Lewis.

After recording the "Hall of Faith," the author of Hebrews wrote, "Since we also have such a large cloud of witnesses surrounding us, let us lay aside every hindrance and the sin that so easily ensnares us. Let us run with endurance the race that lies before us" (Heb. 12:1). As you live your story, you are following in the wake of Christians who have gone before you. You are also building your own legacy of faithfulness.

> God doesn't want you to be the next Moses; He's calling you to be you.

Leaving a legacy of faith doesn't always mean becoming world-famous. It simply means being faithful to Jesus's calling on your life. God doesn't want you to be the next Moses; He's calling you to be you. Find inspiration in the lives of the Christian heroes who preceded you, but live your own story. Live in a way that encourages and challenges those who follow behind you.

DISCOVER

Who are some older Christians in your own life whom you respect? In what ways do these people inspire you to live your own life well?

What is your reputation? If people around you described you in just a few words, what would they say? Are you satisfied or disappointed by this description?

ACT

Which older Christians in your life came to mind when you considered the question above? Reach out to them this week. Arrange to grab lunch together or call or text them. Thank them for the example they've set and ask if they would pray for you as you strive to live your own story of faith well.

Day 53

YOUNG HEROES

*Don't let anyone despise your youth, but set an example for the
believers in speech, in conduct, in love, in faith, and in purity.*
— 1 Timothy 4:12 (ESV)

EXPLORE

Teenager Meg Murry and her siblings combat the darkness in
A Wrinkle in Time; Moana saves her island by restoring the Heart of
Te Fiti; Anne of Green Gables is an orphan who bravely stands up for
her friends; Miles Morales faces mutant villains as Spider-Man while
also dealing with the social pressures of high school;
Luke Skywalker wants to become a Jedi like his father,
even though his uncle wants him to stay home.[5]
What connects these heroes? They are young people
who answer the "call to adventure," often despite the
doubts of adults.

> If God has called
> you, then you
> can be confident
> in your mission,
> regardless of
> your age.

Many of the most celebrated heroes in literature
and cinema are young. The "coming-of-age" story
is one of the most widely told versions of the hero's
journey. Throughout the Bible, God demonstrates
that the call to adventure is not just for the older
generations. David, Mary, Samuel, Jeremiah, and Esther were all young people
called by God to an important task.

Another young person in the Bible is Timothy. His mother was a Jewish
believer, but his father was a Greek. It is likely that Timothy's father was not a
believer or had died, so his mother and grandmother passed their faith down
to him (see 2 Tim. 1:5). Then, one day, he received a call to adventure from a

herald who would become his mentor: the apostle Paul (see Acts 16:1-3). We can only imagine the wide-eyed wonder Timothy felt when Paul, the fearless and famous missionary, chose him to join in that mission!

Over the course of many adventures, they developed a special bond. Paul wrote, "[Timothy] has served with me in the gospel ministry like a son with a father" (Phil. 2:22). Yet Paul knew Timothy would ultimately continue his adventure on his own. Paul challenged Timothy to stay true to the gospel of Jesus: "But as for you, continue in what you have learned and firmly believed . . . from infancy you have known the sacred Scriptures, which are able to give you wisdom for salvation through faith in Christ Jesus" (2 Tim. 3:14-15).

When Timothy was a young pastor, some older people in his church struggled to take him seriously. Paul encouraged him, "Don't let anyone despise your youth, but set an example for the believers in speech, in conduct, in love, in faith, and in purity" (1 Tim. 4:12). Timothy's youth did not prevent him from being a leader. In fact, he set an example for the older generation.

Do you ever feel too young to be a hero? Many people throughout history have felt the same way. But God can use your life as an example. Wisdom has no age requirement. Young people can be wise, and old people foolish. What matters is the source of wisdom: God and His Word (see 2 Tim. 3:16-17). If you are young, then God still has much to do in your life. But you don't have to wait to share what He has already done in you.

We typically think of a wise mentor figure as an old man with a long gray beard. But even young heroes often use the lessons they've learned to inspire others. Don't stop growing or learning, but don't doubt yourself either. If God has called you, then you can be confident in your mission, regardless of your age. Lead the charge and set a godly example for others to follow.

DISCOVER

Do you ever wish people would trust you with greater challenges? How can you live so that you can be trusted with greater challenges?

_____

_____

_____

_____

_____

What opportunities do you have to set an example of faith and wisdom for the adults in your life?

_____

_____

_____

_____

ACT

Let an adult (such as a teacher, boss, parent, or pastor) know that you would like to take on more responsibility. Use this opportunity to set an example for them by the way you live out your faith. Ask God to give you the wisdom to "go the extra mile" and surprise the adults in your life who may have low expectations of the younger generation.

Day 54

GOODBYES

At my first defense, no one stood by me, but everyone deserted
me. . . . But the Lord stood with me and strengthened me.
— 2 Timothy 4:16-17

EXPLORE

Friendships are forged along the journey as characters face challenges, suffer defeats, and regroup to claim victory as a team. Fellow travelers see the hero in good times and bad, which creates an intimate bond. These relationships are special, but they are not always meant to last forever. The hero's journey is about what heroes gain as well as what they leave behind.

At the end of the day, the hero must complete the journey with or without allies and mentors. Due to the perilous nature of each quest, goodbyes are inevitable. In *Dune*, Paul Atreides must continue after his father's assassination; Harry Potter loses friends and mentors leading up to his final confrontation with Voldemort; Frodo experiences betrayal at the hands of Boromir, and the Fellowship of the Ring is broken.[6] Part of what strengthens heroes for their final great test (what Christopher Vogler calls "Approaching the Inmost Cave"[7]) is dealing with loss, whether death, betrayal, or simply diverging paths.

The same is true in your faith journey. God will bless you along the way with mentors, allies, and friends. Not all of these companions will complete the journey with you. The apostle Paul had many partners in his missionary travels, but few of them remained with him. Near the end of his life, he felt the weight of loss. From a prison cell, he wrote to Timothy, "Make every effort to come to me soon, because Demas has deserted me, since he loved this present world, and has gone to Thessalonica. Crescens has gone to Galatia, Titus to Dalmatia. Only Luke is with me" (2 Tim. 4:9-11).

> Although people in your life will inevitably come and go, God will remain with you until the end of your journey.

Paul's fellow traveler Luke (the author of the books of Luke and Acts), was the only one who remained by Paul's side. Some, like Titus (to whom Paul wrote the book of Titus) and Timothy were continuing their own faith journeys in different places. Others, like Demas, had turned away from Paul and their faith. Demas had once been included with Luke as a ministry partner (see Philem. 24; Col. 4:14), but he had been corrupted by a love for things that were inconsistent with God's calling.

Some companions' paths may align with yours for a time before veering off in other directions. People move or move on. Life events, like graduations, often break up "fellowships." Sometimes we face the death of a friend or mentor. Other times we experience the pain of betrayal from a former ally.

Although people in your life will inevitably come and go, God will remain with you until the end of your journey. Paul experienced a lot of "goodbyes" in his life, but he could confidently declare "the Lord stood with me and strengthened me, so that I might fully preach the word and all the Gentiles might hear it" (2 Tim. 4:17).

Don't fear the inevitable goodbyes. They are a natural part of life, as people appear in your story for a few chapters before continuing in their own direction. While goodbyes may be sad, they are necessary as God moves you to the next stage of your journey where many new allies, friends, and mentors await. Hold fast to your friends, but trust God when He wants to bring new people into your life. Above all, even when it feels like all others have abandoned you, remember that God will go with you to the very end.

DISCOVER

Who have you had to say "goodbye" to on your journey so far? What was the hardest part about that parting?

Who are you most afraid of losing? Why?

ACT

Even though people may only be in our life for a few chapters, it's important to make the most of the time we have together. Think of some people in your life who are important to you right now. Take time today to let them know what they mean to you through a conversation, a note, a text, or some other form of communication. Tell them specifically why they are special to you. We promise, they will appreciate hearing what you have to say!

Day 55

BECOMING A STORYTELLER

*"Go, therefore, and make disciples of all nations,
baptizing them in the name of the Father and of
the Son and of the Holy Spirit, teaching them to
observe everything I have commanded you. And
remember, I am with you always, to the end of the age."*
— Matthew 28:19-20

EXPLORE

Good stories are meant to be retold and shared. When we're blown away by an amazing movie, we often want to watch it again with people who haven't experienced it yet. When we finish a captivating book, we lend it to our friends and nag them to read it so we can discuss it with them. Encountering a great story is always enjoyable, but there is something thrilling about sharing the experience with others. Some beloved stories are retold in many forms. It's estimated that there are more than one hundred adaptations of Charles Dickens' holiday classic, *A Christmas Carol.*[9] Each version, though unique, maintains the essence of the original tale.

As we explored at the beginning of this journey, stories require a storyteller. As you live out the story God has for you, He is calling you to become a storyteller as well.

Jesus's disciples experienced a lot in a short time span. Their understanding of the world was flipped upside down. They witnessed miracles, faced violent opposition, and watched as their leader was killed and then resurrected. In fact, John shares in his Gospel that they saw Jesus do many things that aren't recorded, because "not even the world itself could contain the books that would be written" (John 21:25). They had witnessed a lot and had

> Your personal part in that narrative helps people realize this story was not only important two thousand years ago—it is also relevant today.

many stories to tell. One of Jesus's final commands to them was to do exactly that: go into all the world and share the story.

Notice that Jesus didn't call them to become traveling entertainers, pleasing crowds with thrilling tales of what they had seen. Jesus told them to "make disciples of all nations, baptizing them in the name of the Father and of the Son and of the Holy Spirit" (Matt. 28:19). Jesus wanted them to share about Him and to help others experience Him. Paul wrote, "How, then, can they call on him they have not believed in? And how can they believe without hearing about him? And how can they hear without a preacher?" (Rom. 10:14). One of the best ways to encourage others to embark on their own faith journey is to share your experience.

What have you witnessed God do in your life? The most important story you can share is the gospel. But your personal part in that narrative helps people realize this story was not only important two thousand years ago—it is also relevant today. Don't be afraid to tell others about your experiences. If God has been working in your life, then you have stories to tell. How has God guided you through difficult circumstances? When has He empowered you to do something scary that you never believed you could do? Has God ever called you to make a decision that seemed crazy in the moment, but looking back you recognize that it was part of His perfect plan? Have you ever experienced God's peace, even while others attacked you? These experiences are all part of your journey. Tell these stories to challenge and encourage others.

Great tales should be shared and retold. Tell others the ultimate story about what Jesus accomplished on the cross, but also share about your personal experiences with God. Help them understand that the God who journeys with you is inviting them to embark on an adventure that will change their life forever.

DISCOVER

The most important story we can tell is the gospel. How confident do you feel sharing this story with others? Why?

What have been the most significant moments in your faith journey so far?

ACT

Take a few minutes to write out some details from three of the "significant moments" in your answer above. Look for an opportunity today or this week to share these stories with others.

Day 56

THE STORY ISN'T OVER

"This is eternal life: that they may know you, the only true God, and the one you have sent — Jesus Christ."
— John 17:3

EXPLORE

ost romantic comedies and many Disney movies end after the two main characters finally end up together, presumably to live "happily ever after." Some films, like *Shrek* and *Disenchanted*, spoof the fairy-tale genre by asking the question, "What happens after happily ever after?" Are there more adventures to be had once characters return from a hero's journey? Rom-coms usually don't showcase much growth and maturity in the relationship. Hollywood often assumes the exciting part is falling in love, not staying in love. Yet, even after the initial thrills, life continues to offer invitations to new adventures.

> No matter how far you have gone on your journey with God, new adventures still await that will take you even further.

Jesus spoke to His disciples about "eternal life." He wasn't just talking about living for a long time. In fact, movies about immortality typically depict it as a burden or curse. The characters in stories who attempt to cheat death don't necessarily gain happiness; they just discover longevity. When Bilbo Baggins finds the One Ring, it grants him an unnaturally long life but leaves him feeling like "butter spread over too much bread." [10] Who wants to be miserable forever?

The "eternal life" Jesus spoke of was of a certain quality (see John 17:3). It offers a chance to know God as He intended. To "know" is not just "to know about" but to be in a relationship. In other words, abundant life is found when we know God deeply and personally through Jesus. Jesus said, "I am the way, the truth, and the life. No one comes to the Father except through me" (John 14:6). Introductions are fun, but they are only the beginning. The relationship becomes deeper as we invest time and effort into it. Healthy relationships grow.

No matter how far you have gone on your journey with God, new adventures still await that will take you even further. Jesus, speaking metaphorically, said that He is "the vine" and that we are "branches" (John 15:5). If we stay connected to Him, we will "bear much fruit." He also said, "[The Father] prunes every branch that produces fruit so that it will produce more fruit" (15:2). Even if we are "bearing fruit" like a healthy branch should, God desires for us to continue growing so we produce more fruit. How does the Father "prune" us to make us more fruitful? Often by leading us on another journey with Him.

Are you growing in your relationship with God? If you find that you have become stagnant, perhaps another "call to adventure" is around the corner. No matter how far you have come, you haven't even begun to learn all there is to know about God.

The hero's journey is not typically a straight line with a definite beginning and conclusion. Most often when it's portrayed visually, it takes the form of a circle. The journey leads heroes back to where they started. But life doesn't end there. Heroes are now ready to begin the next adventure.

What journey are you currently taking with God? Where are you on that quest? Do you feel as though a new tale is about to unfold? What an exciting place to be! God always has more for you to experience.

DISCOVER

What is the evidence that a relationship is growing in depth and maturity? Is there any evidence that your relationship with God is growing? Why or why not?

Is a "happily ever after" ending realistic? Why or why not?

ACT

If you call yourself a Christian, think back to when you first decided to commit your life to Jesus. Take five minutes to write a brief summary of your walk with Jesus since you first became a Christian. What significant moments did you include? What lessons have you learned along the way? What would you like to see in the next chapters of your faith journey?

Day 57

WAY STATION

PART 8:
THE RETURN

Think back on your journey (not just with this book, but as a follower of
Jesus). What have you gained along the way? How can these "elixirs" be
used to bless others?

Wisdom:	Skill:
What was gained:	*What was gained:*
How it can bless others:	*How it can bless others:*

Purpose:	Accomplishment:
What was gained:	*What was gained:*
How it can bless others:	*How it can bless others:*

Scan the QR code or go to
lifeway.com/godheroesdragons to watch
the video for Part 8: The Return.

173

CONCLUSION

Day 58

NOT YET . . .

He will wipe away every tear from their eyes. Death will be
no more; grief, crying, and pain will be no more, because the
previous things have passed away.
— Revelation 21:4

EXPLORE

ith a good story, we're sad to leave characters behind when the tale ends. Star-crossed lovers finally marry; the cowboy rides off into the sunset; the custodian turns the gym lights off after the underdog team wins and the crowds go home. This portion of the story has ended, but for the characters, life goes on. Our imagination soars as we wonder what those characters may have experienced after we close the last page, turn off the TV, or leave the theater. It's hard to say goodbye to a world we've come to love. But eventually every story must end.

Throughout the pages of this book, we've explored the exciting reality that your story is part of a bigger narrative that God has been unfolding since the beginning of time. As with all stories, yours will end too. The Bible gives us a picture of the end: the final book in the Bible is called Revelation. Much about this book is confusing, strange, and unknown, but it provides an amazing picture of God's final victory over the sin that has marred the world:

"Then I saw a new heaven and a new earth, for the first heaven and the first earth had passed away,

> As Christians, our journeys will eventually lead us to one final joyous conclusion . . . but not yet. Until then, keep moving forward.

and the sea was no more. And I saw the holy city, a new Jerusalem, coming down out of heaven from God, prepared as a bride adorned for her husband. And I heard a loud voice from the throne saying, 'Behold, the dwelling place of God is with man. He will dwell with them, and they will be his people, and God himself will be with them as their God. He will wipe away every tear from their eyes, and death shall be no more, neither shall there be mourning, nor crying, nor pain anymore, for the former things have passed away'" (Rev. 21:1-4).

In a way, this passage might be considered the Bible's "happily ever after." Our imaginations can hardly fathom the life we will experience with God and each other in heaven after our earthly stories have ended. It will be the start of a whole new adventure, a return to the intimacy humans once enjoyed with God in Eden before it was ravaged by sin. Knowing that this glorious future awaits us can encourage us to continue moving forward now.

The Oscar-winning film *Gladiator* follows the story of a Roman general named Maximus who was betrayed and became a slave. He was sold and forced to battle others in the arena to stay alive. He ultimately achieved greatness despite his lowly position and made deep friendships on the journey. At the end of the story, after Maximus dies, his friend and fellow gladiator Juba, who has been set free, speaks these words to him: "Now we are free. I will see you again. But not yet, not yet . . ."[1]

If you are a follower of Jesus, then your ultimate destination, heaven, should be a source of great comfort. We know where we are headed, but we are not there yet. Others have gone before us, and we will see them again one day. What should we do in the meantime? The apostle Paul said it well: "One thing I do: Forgetting what is behind and reaching forward to what is ahead, I pursue as my goal the prize promised by God's heavenly call in Christ Jesus" (Phil. 3:13-14).

As Christians, our journeys will eventually lead us to one final joyous conclusion . . . but not yet. Until then, keep moving forward. Your next hero's journey awaits.

DISCOVER

In what ways can our confidence in our ultimate destination encourage and strengthen us to keep moving forward?

_____

_____

_____

_____

_____

_____

_____

ACT

You've reached the conclusion of this book, but not the end of your journey. Take a moment to pray. In a symbolic gesture, you may want to hold out your hands, palms up, and offer this prayer to God: *God, thank You for the journey You have me on and that I will one day arrive in heaven with You. Until that day, my open hands represent my commitment to give everything to You. They also represent my commitment to accept everything You have for me on the journey ahead. Please lead me. I commit myself to follow You. Amen.*

Scan the QR code or go to lifeway.com/godheroesdragons to watch the video for the Conclusion.

GROUP GUIDE

Leading a group?

Whether a large or small group, we have what you need to lead a group of students through *God, Heroes, and Everyday Dragons*. Visit **lifeway.com/godheroesdragons** for free leader downloads, including Character Profile PDF, promotional resources, and more.

Students can use this book on their own, but there is great value in walking together as a group through the ideas and content in this Bible study. The following is a guide for a weekly meeting with students who are reading *God, Heroes, and Everyday Dragons*. Feel free to personalize this to fit the needs of your group.

Group Time Schedule:

- Icebreaker (5 minutes)
- Recap the session (5 minutes)
- Watch video from authors Mike and Daniel Blackaby together (3 minutes)
- Work on character profile (10–15 minutes)
- Discussion questions (20–25 minutes)
- Close in prayer (5 minutes)

Tips to Leading a Group:

- Do the study alongside students. Make notes as you work through the days and bring those thoughts to your group time.
- Print copies of the Character Profile and make available for students at each meeting as needed.

- Gather any supplies for icebreakers before the group meets.
- Cue up the video with Mike and Daniel Blackaby prior to students gathering for group time.
- Don't be afraid of silence. Students need time to process and think especially after a deep question.
- Record prayer requests and follow up.

Part 1: The Storyteller

Icebreaker: Ask group members to each share one favorite story (this can be from any storytelling medium, such as novels, movies, video games, comic books, or television) and why those stories are their favorites.

Recap: God is the divine Storyteller and Author of all of our stories. He is good and He can be trusted to guide us in a way that is good. He has been weaving together a story from the beginning of time and we are characters in His divine narrative.

Video: Part 1: "The Storyteller"

Discussion Questions:

- How have you experienced God as the divine Storyteller in your life? How has He proven Himself to you as a trustworthy author in your story?
- What evidence have you seen that God is active in the world?
- When have you felt something should go differently in your life than how it unfolded? How has God walked with you through that experience or situation?

Close in prayer.

Part 2: The Plot

Icebreaker: Give each student in your group a piece of paper and a pen. Ask each student to write a one sentence plot summary of a very well known movie. For example, "An underwater princess longs to be where the people are." That would be a summary of *The Little Mermaid*.[1] Allow students to read their one sentence plot summaries and let the other students in the group guess the movie.

Recap: There are two major plot twists in the story of humanity. The first was when we fell into sin, recounted in Genesis 3. This changed the course of the human story forever. The second happened when God sent His only Son, Jesus, to the world to reverse the effects of sin by dying on a cross and rising again from the dead three days later. This plot twist is where we find our meaning and inspiration in life.

Video: Part 2: "The Plot"

Discussion Questions:

- How have you seen or experienced the plot twist of humanity's fall into sin the most vividly in your life's story?
- Discuss the story of the gospel: Who is the most important person in the story? What did He do that changed everything? How does this impact your life? How would you explain this story to someone else?
- How have you seen the true story of the gospel of Jesus change the course of someone's life? How can you share the story of Jesus more often in your own life's story?

Close in prayer.

Part 3: A Call to Adventure

Icebreaker: Ask students this question: "If your phone rang and you looked down to see who it was, if that person calling you could be anyone who has ever lived, who would you want that phone call to be from and why?" Let all of them answer and explain their answers.

Recap: As followers of Jesus, we have received a call from God. It's not a call to fame and fortune like some of the calls the heroes in our favorite stories receive. No, it's a call to the adventurous unknown. It's a call to place your faith in the loving hands of our God who has provided salvation to us through Jesus. It is a call to follow Jesus wherever He leads. It is a call to lay down our lives and obey His commands. It's not easy, but it's the best life you could ever imagine.

Video: Part 3: "A Call to Adventure"

Discussion Questions:

- A big part of answering the call God has for your life is your willingness to say yes to Him. When have you said yes to God and what was the result?
- How have you experienced a difference in your life following Jesus as opposed to following the ways of the world?
- Part of answering God's call to adventure is to shine a light for others to see. Who has shined a light in your life and how did them answering God's call impact you and influence your willingness to follow God's call in your own life?

Close in prayer.

Part 4: Companions & Guides

Icebreaker: Write a series of questions and present them to your group. These questions should involve their choosing someone else from the group to help them. For example, "If you were lost in the woods, which person would you trust to help you find your way home?" or "If you were trying to convince your parents to let you stay out past curfew, which person do you think could come closest to convincing them?" Come up with six to eight questions like this to ask the group. Don't ask questions that would make fun of students or intentionally embarrass anyone. Keep it fun, positive, and encouraging.

Recap: On our life's journey we need some things that can help us along the way, not the least of which are friends, the Holy Spirit, the Bible, prayer, and the church. These people and things help guide us, hold us accountable, give us counsel, and know which paths to take. God put these people and things in our lives so that we can receive the help we need as we navigate our journey. We are also called to be a friend to others on their life's journey as well.

Video: Part 4: "Companions & Guides"

Discussion Questions:

- When you think about the word "community," what comes to mind? In what ways does God provide community for us in our lives?
- The Bible describes the Holy Spirit in many ways: counselor, guide, helper, among many other things. Which role has the Holy Spirit played in your life most prominently?
- What has helped you learn how to spend time in God's Word? What is an area where you need to grow in your time in the Bible?

Close in prayer.

Part 5: Character Arc

Icebreaker: Give each student a piece of paper and a pen. Ask students: "If someone were to make a movie of your life, who would you cast to play you?" Collect their responses. Then, read out the actors and let the others in the group guess who each of them are playing. Again, keep it positive and encouraging. Steer the game away from students making fun of each other.

Recap: In most stories, the main characters don't end the story the same people they were when they began their journeys. The same will be true for us as followers of Christ. In fact, the point of our journey following Jesus is to grow and change along the way. We are unfinished products, and God develops our character as we walk with Him. Our identity is rooted in Him, and as we grow, our character is shaped and developed, and we mature as believers. This is what a successful hero's journey looks like in the life of a follower of Christ.

Video: Part 5: "Character Arc"

Discussion Questions:

- No matter how long you've been a follower of Christ, what is the biggest way you are different now from when you started your journey with Jesus?
- In what way can you see most clearly that God is molding and shaping you to be more like Jesus?
- The world wants us to put our identities in so many different things: our race, sexuality, social status, and more. God calls us to find ourselves in Him. In the midst of all the competing voices you hear from day to day, how do you remind yourself that you belong to Him?

Close in prayer.

Part 6: Crossing the Threshold

Icebreaker: Bring a gallon of water to the group meeting. Ask if any volunteers would be willing to hold the gallon of water straight out in front of them. Say to your chosen volunteer, "You can probably hold this for a while, but eventually your muscles will give out and you'll drop it." Let another volunteer come up and help that student hold the gallon of water. Here we see an image of what it means to cross the threshold. There will be moments when we want to quit. Those are the moments when we have to trust that God will carry us and help us bear the weight of the task He has called us to.

Recap: Sometimes the road gets rough along the journey of life. Sometimes you might feel like it's more than you can bear. This is the moment of decision or crossing the threshold. Will you keep going, or will you turn back? This is where faith comes in. Faith takes what cannot be seen and puts it into practice. Jesus doesn't call us to do things we could have done on our own. He calls us to rely upon Him and do things through faith that only He can do.

Video: Part 6: "Crossing the Threshold"

Discussion Questions:

- When has the journey gotten difficult for you in your walk with Jesus? How did you stay on the path, even though it was difficult?
- When has God called you to do something that seemed strange? How were you able to obey, even though you didn't see the whole picture of what God was seeking to accomplish through you?
- How do you stay in step with Jesus and not get out in front of Him?

Close in prayer.

Part 7: Trials & Adversity

Icebreaker: Search the internet for mazes of varying degrees of difficulty. Print them and pass them out to your group. Give students pens/pencils and set a timer for thirty seconds for them to complete their mazes. Sometimes we will face trials and adversity that we can navigate easily. Other times the challenges will be great. In all instances, we must walk with Jesus and stay in step with His Spirit who lives in us.

Recap: In every story there is conflict. The greatest conflict in our Christian journey is sin—our own and others'. Many times, you will struggle, or people will stand in your way to oppose you, challenging your faith and seeking to knock you down. In every instance of conflict and opposition Jesus faced, He answered with love. None of us are perfect, but we have a perfect Savior who desires to show us the way through the trials and adversity.

Video: Part 7: "Trials & Adversity"

Discussion Questions:

- How is admitting that we need help a good thing? How can confessing sin in our lives be the very thing that sets us free?
- So often we think of trials and adversity as bad. When has a challenge been a good thing in your life?
- How do you remind yourself that you are not alone on this journey? When was a time you were very aware of the presence of the Holy Spirit as you went through something difficult?

Close in prayer.

Part 8: The Return

Icebreaker: Ask students: What has been their biggest takeaway from this study? Ask if anyone would be willing to share the most impactful part of filling out their Character Profile.

Recap: One of the most important elements of our journey with Jesus is to pass along what He has taught us. Our stories operate in cycles. Sometimes God has new challenges for us; other times we are in what seems to be a holding pattern. No matter where He takes us in the story of our lives, no matter who comes and goes, God will be with us every step of the way.

Video: Part 8: "The Return"

Discussion Questions:

- Share about someone who has meant a lot to you in your Christian journey who is either not in your life anymore or has moved to a place where you cannot be in close contact as much.
- What is something that you feel God is uniquely calling you to do? How is His calling on your life different from someone else's?
- What new adventure is ahead of you? How will you prepare to walk along that road faithfully with God?

Close in prayer.

NOTES

REFERENCES

Introduction

1. J. R. R. Tolkien, personal communication, September 19, 1931, quoted in Humphrey Carpenter, *J. R. R. Tolkien: A Biography* (New York: Houghton Mifflin Company, 1977), 151.

2. Joseph Campbell, *The Hero with a Thousand Faces* (New York: Pantheon, 1949), 23.

3. J. R. R. Tolkien, *The Two Towers* (London: George Allen & Unwin, 1954; New York: Del Rey, 2018), 362. Citations refer to the Del Rey edition.

Part 1 — The Storyteller

1. Nick Collins, "Monkeys at Typewriters 'Close to Reproducing Shakespeare,'" The Daily Telegraph, September 26, 2011, accessed August 24, 2018, http://www.telegraph.co.uk/technology/news/8789894/Monkeys-at-typewriters-close-to-reproducing-Shakespeare.html.

2. *Star Wars: A New Hope,* directed by George Lucas (San Francisco, CA: Lucasfilm, 1977).

3. Charles Dickens. *A Tale of Two Cities* (London: Chapman & Hall, 1859; New York: Signet Classics, 2007), 7. Citation refers to the Signet edition.

4. George Orwell. *1984* (London: Secker & Warburg, 1949; New York: Berkley, 2017), 1. Citation refers to the Berkley edition.

5. "War and Peace Vol. 1 & 2, by Leo Tolstoy (Paperback)" (product page), Wildside Press, accessed May 31, 2023, https://wildsidepress.com/war-and-peace-vol-1-2-by-leo-tolstoy-trade-pb/.

6. "Unofficial Harry Potter Character Compendium" (product page), Asia Books, accessed May 31, 2023, https://www.asiabooks.com/unofficial-harry-potter-character-compendium-263039.html.

7. Vanessa Armstrong, "Study Suggests Game of Thrones Books Are Engaging Because They Mimic Real Life (Well, Minus the Dragons)," SyFy, November 4, 2020, https://www.syfy.com/syfy-wire/scientific-study-game-of-thrones-why-engaging.

8. Liberty Hardy, "A Cast of Thousands: The Wheel of Time Character Guide," Audible Blog, November 19, 2021, https://www.audible.com/blog/article-the-wheel-of-time-character-guide.

9. *Raiders of the Lost Ark,* directed by Steven Spielberg (Hollywood, CA: Paramount, 1981).

10. Tolkien, *The Two Towers*, 363.

Part 2 — The Plot

1. C. S. Lewis, *The Collected Letters of C. S. Lewis: Family Letters 1905-1931*, edited by Walter Hooper (New York: HarperCollins, 2004), 977.

2. *Avatar*, directed by James Cameron (Manhattan Beach, CA: Lightstorm Entertainment, 2009).

3. *Jurassic Park*, directed by Steven Spielberg (Universal City, CA: Universal Pictures, 1993).

4. Kenneth O. Gangel and Stephen J. Bramer, *Genesis*, ed. Max Anders, Holman Old Testament Commentary (B&H Publishing Group, 2002), 28.

5. *Animal Crossing: New Horizons* (Nintendo, 2020), Switch.

6. *The Legend of Zelda: Link's Awakening* (Nintendo, 1993), Game Boy.

Part 3 — A Call to Adventure

1. C. S. Lewis, *The Voyage of the Dawn Treader* (London: Geoffrey Bles, 1952).

2. Joseph Campbell, *Reflections on the Art of Living: A Joseph Campbell Companion*, edited by Diane K. Osbon (New York: HarperPerennial, 1991), 77.

3. *The Lord of the Rings: The Two Towers,* directed by Peter Jackson (Burbank, CA: New Line Cinema, 2002).

4. *New Hope*, Lucas.

5. Joseph Campbell. *The Hero with a Thousand Faces*, 3rd ed. (Novato, CA: New World Library, 2008), 23.

6. *New Hope*, Lucas.; *The Matrix*, directed by the Wachowskies (Burbank, CA: Warner Brothers, 1999).

7. *The Lego Movie,* written and directed by Phil Lord and Christopher Miller (Burbank, CA: Warner Animation Group, 2014).

188

8. *Aladdin,* directed by Ron Clements and John Musker (Burbank, CA: Walt Disney, 1992).

9. *Iron Man,* directed by Jon Favreau, (Hollywood, CA: Paramount Pictures, 2008).

10. *New Hope,* Lucas.

11. J. R. R. Tolkien, *The Fellowship of the Ring* (London: George Allen & Unwin, 1954; New York: Del Rey, 2018), 55-56. Citations refer to the Del Rey edition.

Part 4

1. K. A. Matthews, *Genesis 1-11:26,* vol. 1A, The New American Commentary (Nashville: Broadman & Holman Publishers, 1996), 213, Logos edition.

2. Mary Shelley, *Frankenstein: or, The Modern Prometheus* (London, 1818).

3. *The Empire Strikes Back,* directed by Irvin Kershner (San Francisco, CA: Lucasfilm, 1980).

4. Lois Lowry, *The Giver* (Boston: Houghton Mifflin, 1993).

5. *Pinocchio,* directed by Ben Sharpsteen and Hamilton Luske (Burbank, CA: Walt Disney Productions, 1940).

6. Robert Louis Stevenson, *Treasure Island* (London, 1883).

7. "Best Selling Book," Guinness World Records, accessed June 9, 2023, https://www.guinnessworldrecords.com/world-records/best-selling-book-of-non-fiction.

8. *Avengers: Endgame,* directed by Anthony and Joe Russo (Burbank, CA: Marvel Studios, 2010).

9. *Lost,* season 1, episode 5, "White Rabbit," directed by Kevin Hooks, written by Jeffrey Lieber, J. J. Abrams, and Damon Lindelof, aired October 20, 2004, ABC, (Santa Monica, CA: Bad Robot Productions).

Part 5

1. *The Hobbit: An Unexpected Journey,* directed by Peter Jackson (Burbank, CA: New Line Cinema, 2013).

2. Brandon Sanderson, *The Way of Kings* (New York: Tor Books, 2010).

3. "Number of Books Published Per Year,"

Wordsrated, February 2, 2022, https://wordsrated.com/number-of-books-published-per-year-2021/.

4. "About Spotify," Spotify — For the Record, accessed May 31, 2023, https://newsroom.spotify.com/company-info/.

5. Online Etymology Dictionary, s.v. "poesy (n.)," accessed June 12, 2023, https://www.etymonline.com/word/poesy.

6. Bible Hub, s.v. "4161. poiéma," accessed June 12, 2023, https://biblehub.com/greek/4161.htm.

7. *Toy Story,* directed by John Lasseter (Pixar Animation Studios and Walt Disney Pictures, 1995).

8. C. S. Lewis, *The Chronicles of Narnia* series (London: Geoffrey Bles, 1950–1954 [books 1–5]; The Bodley Head, 1955–1956 [books 6–7]).

9. *Spiderman: Homecoming,* directed by John Watts (Culver City, CA: Sony Pictures, 2017.)

10. Ernest Cline, *Ready Player One* (New York: Crown Publishers, 2011).

Part 6

1. Leland Ryken, "10 Things You Should Know About The Pilgrim's Progress," Crossway, October 1, 2019, https://www.crossway.org/articles/10-things-you-should-know-about-pilgrims-progress/.

2. Paul Bunyan, *The Pilgrim's Progress* (London: 1678).

3. Joseph Campbell, *The Hero with a Thousand Faces,* Commemorative Edition (Princeton: Princeton University Press, 2004), 71.

4. *The Wizard of Oz,* directed by Victor Fleming (Beverly Hills, CA: Metro-Goldwyn-Mayer, 1939).

5. Campbell, *Hero* (2008), 64, 67–68.

6. J. K. Rowling, *Harry Potter and the Chamber of Secrets* (New York: Scholastic, 1999).

7. *New Hope,* Lucas.

8. *The Dark Knight Rises,* directed by Christofher Nolan (Burbank, CA: Warner Brothers, 2012).

9. C. S. Lewis, *The Problem of Pain* (London: Centenary Press & Geoffrey Bles Ltd., 1940;

New York: HarperCollins, 1996), 116. Citation refers to the HarperCollins edition.

Part 7

1. Campbell, *Hero* (2004), 227.

2. *The Legend of Zelda* (Nintendo, 1986), Nintendo Entertainment System.

3. John Bunyan, *The Pilgrim's Progress* (London, 1678; New York: Barnes & Noble Classics, 2005), 55. Citation refers to the Barnes & Noble edition.

4. Campbell, *Hero* (2004), 227.

5. *The Lord of the Rings: The Return of the King*, directed by Peter Jackson (Burbank, CA: New Line Cinema, 2003).

6. Friedrich Nietzsche, *Twilight of the Idols, or, How to Philosophize with a Hammer* (Leipzig, 1888), quoted in *The Portable Nietzsche*, edited by Walter Kaufmann (New York: Penguin, 1976), 467.

7. *The Dark Knight*, directed by Christopher Nolan (Burbank, CA: Warner Brothers, 2008).

8. *Empire*, Kersnher; *Return of the Jedi*, directed by Richard Marquand (San Rafael, CA: Lucasfilm, 1983).

Part 8

1. Miguel de Cervantes, *Don Quixote* (Madrid: Francisco de Robles, 1605 [part 1] and 1615 [part 2]).

2. Christopher Vogler, *The Writer's Journey: Mythic Structure for Writers* (Studio City, CA: Michael Wiese Productions, 1998).

3. *Two Towers*, Jackson.

4. *Star Wars: The Force Awakens*, directed by J. J. Abrams (San Francisco, CA: Lucasfilm, 2015).

5. Madeline L'Engle, *A Wrinkle in Time* (New York: Ariel Books, 1962); *Moana*, directed by John Musker and Ron Clements (Burbank, CA: Walt Disney Animation Studios, 2016); L. M. Montgomery, *Anne of Green Gables* (Boston: L. C. Page, 1908); *Spider-Man: Into the Spider-Verse*, directed by Bob Peersichetti, Peter Ramsey, and Rodney Rothman (Culver City, CA: Columbia Pictures, 2018); *New Hope*, Lucas.

6. Frank Herbert, *Dune* (Boston: Chilton, 1965); J. K. Rowling, *Harry Potter and the Deathly Hallows* (London: Bloomsbury, 2007); Tolkien, *Fellowship*.

7. Christopher Vogler, *The Writer's Journey: Mythic Structure for Writers* (Studio City, CA: Michael Wiese Productions, 1998).

8. J. R. R. Tolkien, *The Return of the King* (London: George Allen & Unwin, 1955; New York: Del Rey, 2018), 339. Citation refers to the Del Rey edition.

9. "Adaptations," The Dickens Project, UC Santa Cruz, accessed April 23, 2023, https://dickens.ucsc.edu/resources/teachers/carol/adaptations.html

10. *The Lord of the Rings: The Fellowship of the Ring*, directed by Peter Jackson (Burbank, CA: New Line Cinema, 2001).

Conclusion

1. *Gladiator*, directed by Ridley Scott (Universal City, CA: Universal, 2000).

Group Guide

1. *The Little Mermaid*, directed by Rob Marshall (Burbank, CA: Walt Disney Pictures, 2023).